ASVAB
SUCCESS

LearningExpress with Military Expert
Lynn Vincent

NEW YORK

Library of Congress Cataloging-in-Publication Data:
ASVAB success.—1st ed.
      p. cm.
   ISBN 1-57685-386-1 (pbk.)
      1. Armed Services Vocational Aptitude Battery—Study guides.
   2. United States—Armed Forces—Examinations. I. LearningExpress (Organization)

   U408.5 .A847 2001
   355' .00973—dc21

                                                          2001033889

Printed in the United States of America
9 8 7 6 5 4 3 2 1
First Edition

ISBN 1-57685-386-1

For more information or to place an order, contact LearningExpress at:
900 Broadway
Suite 604
New York, NY 10003

Or visit us at:
   www.learnatest.com

GENERAL SCIENCE

This is a subtest of knowledge that measures the physical and biological sciences. Only 25 questions test your abilities in this area. Try these samples:

1. Water is an example of a
   a. crystal.
   b. solid.
   c. gas.
   d. liquid.

2. Substances which hasten chemical reaction time without themselves undergoing changes are called
   a. buffers.
   b. colloids.
   c. reducers.
   d. catalysts.

Answers
1. d
2. d

ARITHMETIC REASONING

This subtest measures your ability to solve arithmetic word problems. This section contains just 30 questions. Here are two examples:

1. If 12 men are needed to run four machines, how many men are needed to run 20 machines?
   a. 20
   b. 48
   c. 60
   d. 80

2. How many 36-passenger buses will it take to carry 144 people?
   a. 3
   b. 4
   c. 5
   d. 6

Answers
1. c
2. b

WORD KNOWLEDGE

This subtest measures your ability to select the correct meaning of words and to identify a synonym (a word that means the same, or nearly the same thing, as the word in the question). You'll answer 35 questions in this subtest. Try these:

1. The wind is *variable* today.
   a. mild
   b. steady
   c. shifting
   d. chilling

2. Rudiments most nearly means
   a. politics
   b. minute details
   c. promotion opportunities
   d. basic methods and procedures

Answers
1. c
2. d

PARAGRAPH COMPREHENSION

This subtest measures your ability to obtain information from written passages. This is a short one: only 15 questions. Here are two examples:

1. Twenty-five percent of all household burglaries can be attributed to unlocked windows or doors. Crime is the result of opportunity plus desire. To prevent crime, it is each individual's responsibility to:
   a. provide the desire.
   b. provide the opportunity.
   c. prevent the desire.
   d. prevent the opportunity.

2. In certain areas, water is so scarce that every attempt is made to conserve it. For instance, on an oasis in the Sahara Desert, the amount of water necessary for each date palm has been carefully determined. How much water is each tree given?
   a. no water at all
   b. water on alternate days
   c. exactly the amount required
   d. water only if it is healthy

Answers
   1. d
   2. c

NUMERICAL OPERATIONS

This is a speed test, so there are more questions—50. This subtest measures your ability to perform arithmetic computations. Try answering these two sample questions as quickly as you can:

1. $3 + 9 =$
   a. 3
   b. 6
   c. 12
   d. 13

2. $\frac{60}{15} =$
   a. 3
   b. 4
   c. 5
   d. 6

Answers
   1. c
   2. b

CODING SPEED

Another speed test, at 84 questions, this one is the longest part of the ASVAB. Coding speed measures your ability to use a key in assigning code numbers to words, or to find a specific number in a table. Each group of questions is based on an answer key that is found at the top of the page. The answer key contains several words, with a number assigned to each word. Each question gives you a word from the key and several choices of numbers. One of the numbers is the one assigned to that word in the answer key. Your job on each question is to identify the number that matches the word in the answer key. This is a speed test, so you should complete the questions as quickly as you can. Here's a sample:

Key:

Green ... 2715	Man 3451	Salt 4586
Hat 1413	Room ... 2864	Tree 5972

Questions:

1. Room
   a. 1413
   b. 2715
   c. 2864
   d. 3451
   e. 4586

2. Green
   (a.) 2715
   b. 2864
   c. 3451
   d. 4586
   e. 5972

3. Tree
   a. 1413
   b. 2715
   c. 3451
   d. 4586
   (e.) 5972

4. Hat
   (a.) 1413
   b. 2715
   c. 3451
   d. 4586
   e. 5972

Answers
   1. c
   2. a
   3. e
   4. a

AUTO AND SHOP INFORMATION

This subtest measures your knowledge of automobiles, tools and shop terminology and practices. It's 25 questions long. Try this sample:

1. A chisel is used for:
   a. prying
   b. cutting
   c. twisting
   (d.) grinding

Answers
   1. b

MATHEMATICS KNOWLEDGE

If it seems like there's a lot of math on the test, don't worry—this book will help you prepare. The 25 questions on this Mathematics Knowledge subtest measure your knowledge of high school mathematics principles. Here are two examples:

1. If 50 percent of $x = 66$, then $x = ?$
   a. 33
   (b.) 66
   c. 99
   d. 132

2. If $x + 6 = 7$, then x is equal to ?
   a. -1
   b. 0
   (c.) 1
   d. $\frac{7}{16}$

Answers
   1. d
   2. c

MECHANICAL COMPREHENSION

This subtest measures your knowledge of mechanical and physical principles. It also checks your ability to visualize how illustrated objects work. This portion of the ASVAB is 25 questions long. Try answering this one:

1. An elevator uses which of the following mechanical devices?
   a. a cable
   b. a pulley
   c. a motor
   (d.) all of the above

Answer

1. d

ELECTRONICS INFORMATION

The final ASVAB subtest is just 20 questions long and measures your knowledge of electricity and electronics. Here is a pair of sample questions:

1. What does the abbreviation A.C. stand for?
   a. additional charge
   b. alternating coil
   c. alternating current
   d. ampere current

2. Which of the following has the least resistance?
   a. wood
   b. iron
   c. rubber
   d. silver

Answers

1. c
2. b

Those are the kinds of questions you can expect on the ASVAB exam. As you can see, it's not hard stuff—just information you've likely run across in high school. Still, it's easy to forget facts you once learned about subjects like electrical current and chemical reactions. That's why it's important to review those knowledge areas. With that said, for the science, mechanical, and electronics portions of the test, we suggest you review chapter summaries found in high school science and auto shop textbooks, or try *ASVAB* (LearningExpress, 2000). This book will take care of the most important part of the ASVAB exam—the AFQT, or Armed Forces Qualification Test.

THE AFQT

The AFQT is both a test-within-a-test and a "composite" test score. While the full ASVAB covers all the subject areas listed above, the AFQT score covers only four "core subjects." The core subjects are Arithmetic Reasoning, Mathematics Knowledge, Paragraph Comprehension, and Word Knowledge. Your AFQT score is derived from these four ASVAB core-subject subtests.

Recruiters and military job "classifiers" use the full ASVAB exam to help recruits decide on military jobs—that's why it's not a "pass/fail" test. But in a sense, you can fail the AFQT. That's because there is a minimum AFQT score that every military recruit must achieve in order to be allowed to enlist in the service. That makes it especially important to spend most of your ASVAB preparation time studying the core subjects.

That's where this book comes in. Read on to learn how LearningExpress will help you score your best on the AFQT.

READING AND VOCABULARY

Reading is the basis of all other learning skills, but many people struggle to read well. Some students did not receive individual teaching at a young age when it was necessary. Others simply did not enjoy reading and, as a result, didn't do enough of it to develop good reading skills.

If you are not reading as well as you think you should, you are not alone. According to the National Assessment of Educational Progress, a significant number of students—as many as a third at some grade levels—are not reaching their reading potential.

However, to succeed in today's world, good reading skills are important. Whether it's reading a repair manual, working at a computer, or just reading the assembly guide for the new stereo you bought, reading is a fundamental skill you use daily.

Military servicemembers do a lot of reading. To advance in rank, servicemembers must read and take tests. To perform their jobs, soldiers, sailors, and airmen read and learn from manuals. To make sure the military work environment remains safe, military personnel read and memorize safety rules.

Servicemembers also are constantly learning new words. This begins the day you arrive in boot camp and never stops. Since military personnel continually try to advance in rank, each level of responsibility brings with it a new set of terms to master.

This book will help you read more effectively. You'll learn to:

- find important facts while reading
- locate main ideas
- sort out fact from opinion
- understand tools used by writers like "cause and effect," "comparing and contrasting," and "logic versus emotion"

This book will also help you expand your vocabulary. You learn to:

- use "root" words to discover word meanings
- define and use common word prefixes and endings
- figure out unfamiliar words without a dictionary

MATHEMATICS

Math is one of those subjects where many students sit in class and think, "Why do I have to learn this? I'm never going to use this stuff." Sometimes that's true: After high school, you may never again in life have to figure out the area of a parallelogram. But wait. You *may* have to calculate the area of a rectangle—a feat that uses the same math skills.

Let's say you need to figure out how much gravel to buy to cover a patch of ground beside your house. The patch measures 100 feet by 9 feet. The labels on the gravel bags say that each bag covers 15 square feet with 2 inches of gravel. If you don't know a little simple geometry, you'd have a tough time figuring out that you need to buy 60 bags of gravel.

Every day, we use math to figure out other simple things: How much change the grocery clerk owes us; how much of a tip to leave at the restaurant; how to double the pancake recipe on the Bisquick™ box.

Math is especially important in the military. Not every servicemember uses math daily, but many military occupational specialties are technical and require a good working knowledge of math. Even non-technical fields require basic math: A cook must calculate measurements. A weather technician has to figure wind speeds and distances. A medical specialist must record and calculate all kinds of critical numbers.

This book will help you:

- review basic operations in addition, subtraction, multiplication, and division
- get ready to tackle fractions, decimals, percents, and word problems
- gain a working knowledge of basic geometry, including lines, angles, triangles, rectangles, squares, and circles.
- refresh your knowledge of math terms

STUDY AND TEST-TAKING SKILLS

Did you ever know anyone in school who studied way less than you, but made better grades? Chances are that person wasn't a genius. Instead, he or she probably learned some basic strategies for studying and taking tests. This book will also help you master basic study and test-taking skills. If you're planning to join the military, those skills will be important. As we've mentioned before, military servicemembers spend significant time studying and taking tests for job training and advancement in rank.

Studying this book will help you:

- calm pre-test jitters
- discover and apply your learning style
- create a "do-able" study plan for the ASVAB and other tests you might take in the future
- remember what you've learned
- score high on multiple choice tests
- increase your chances of guessing right answers when you run into unfamiliar material

With all that help in store for you, the ASVAB should be a snap. And since you're taking the exam, you may be open to considering the military for a single tour, or even a career. Read on to get important information on military jobs and benefits. Making good choices *before* you sign an enlistment contract will improve your chances of enjoying a successful experience in the U.S. armed forces.

MILITARY CAREER OPTIONS

More than 1.2 million people serve in the U.S. armed forces. Every one of them learns "real world" skills that can later transfer into the civilian job market. You can get those skills, too. But first you have to select a specific job, or what the military calls an "occupational specialty." If you decide to join the military, you'll meet with a military personnel specialist called a "classifier." The classifier will tell you what kinds of jobs are available and whether you meet the eligibility requirements for the ones that interest you.

There are more than 150 military occupational specialties to choose from, and you should never jump blindly into any of them. Such a "leap of faith" won't necessarily block future success, but it's better to study and plan a military career track before you enter the service. What kind of work are you interested in? Which service branch offers the most attractive program in that field? Do you qualify for that program? Here is a sampling of what kinds of jobs the military offers:

Human Services

Case Workers

Religious Program Specialists

Media and Public Affairs

Photographic Specialists

Interpreters and Translators

Musicians

Audiovisual and Broadcast Technicians

Broadcast Journalists and Newswriters

Graphic Designers and Illustrators

Healthcare

Medical Care Technicians

Radiologic (X-ray) Technicians

Cardiopulmonary and EEG Technicians

Pharmacy Technicians

Dental Specialists

Physical and Occupational Therapy Specialists

Medical Laboratory Technicians

Medical Record Technicians

Medical Service Technicians

Optometric Technicians

Engineering, Science, and Technical

Communications Equipment Operators

Space Operations Specialists

Ordnance Specialists

Air Traffic Controllers

Radar and Sonar Operators

Meteorological Specialists

Chemical Laboratory Technicians

Radio Intelligence Operators

Non-Destructive Testers

Computer Programmers

Emergency Management Specialists

Environmental Health & Safety Specialists

Intelligence Specialists

Surveying, Mapping, and Drafting Technicians

Administrative

Recruiting Specialists

Personnel Specialists

Postal Specialists

Flight Operations Specialists

Preventive Maintenance Analysts

Legal Specialists and Court Reporters

Administrative Support Specialists

Computer Systems Specialists

Finance and Accounting Specialists

Sales and Stock Specialists

Supply and Warehousing Specialists

Training Specialists and Instructors

Transportation Specialists

Vehicle and Machinery Mechanic

Aircraft Mechanics

Automotive and Heavy Equipment Mechanics

Heating and Cooling Mechanics

Drivers

Marine Engine Mechanics

Powerhouse Mechanics

Electronic and Electrical Equipment Repair

Computer Equipment Repairers

Weapons Maintenance Technicians

Electronic Instrument Repairers

Photographic Equipment Repairers

Precision Instrument Repairers

Ship Electricians

Electrical Products Repairers

Aircraft Electricians

Communications Equipment Repairers

Power Plant Electricians

Radar and Sonar Equipment Repairers

Construction

Construction Equipment Operators

Plumbers and Pipe Fitters

Construction Specialists

Building Electricians

Machine Operator and Precision Work

Welders and Metal Workers

Compressed Gas Technicians

Machinists

Power Plant Operators

Survival Equipment Specialists

Water and Sewage Treatment Plant Operators

Dental and Optical Laboratory Technicians

Printing Specialists

Transportation and Material Handling

Air Crew Members

Cargo Specialists

Flight Engineers

Seamen

Vehicle Drivers

Aircraft Launch and Recovery Specialists

Petroleum Supply Specialists

Quartermasters and Boat Operators

Combat Specialty

Combat Engineers

Special Operations Forces

Tank Crew Members

Infantrymen

Artillery Crew Members

Any of those jobs sound "do-able?" Like something you might enjoy learning and doing for three or four years, or even longer? Read on to learn the smart way to join the military.

THE SMART WAY TO JOIN THE MILITARY

Some books say the first thing you should do before joining the military is go talk with a recruiter. Granted, a recruiter is trained to give you the very latest information on what the military has to offer, but recruiters also have quotas to fill. They must fill certain kinds of jobs with a certain number of "bodies," and they must do so every month—their performance evaluations depend on it. Thus, while recruiters are an important early step in the process of joining the military, your first step should be doing a little advance research.

Here are two good sources of information on the military that won't get you logged permanently in anyone's database:

THE INTERNET

Via the World Wide Web, you can check out military service opportunities without leaving home. Informative websites include the Today's Military website: www.todaysmilitary.com—This military-sponsored information and recruitment site is an excellent source of information on service careers across all branches.

> **Service-Specific Websites:**
> www.goarmy.com
> www.navyjobs.com
> www.airforce.com
> www.marines.com
> www.uscg.mil/jobs/

You do not need to provide any personal information to access the sites above. And they're a great way to explore specific service branch options.

LEARNINGEXPRESS

The Military Advantage (Lynn Vincent, LearningExpress, 2001) is a book that spells out the career and lifetime benefits of a military career. It shows you how to choose the right military occupational specialty, how to pursue a college degree while serving on active duty, and how to market your military job skills for a post-service career.

Advance research will help you with two very important early decisions—which service branch you'd like to join and what kind of job you'd like to have.

VISITING A RECRUITER

After doing some research in the sources listed above, you'll be armed with two things: One, information on what kinds of jobs are available in the service, and two, which service branches you'd like to consider. Now you're ready to visit a recruiter—maybe more than one. You can find recruiters in your local telephone book or via your school guidance counselor. If you live in a remote area, you can find a recruiter near you via the Internet or by dialing 411 for directory assistance.

A service-branch recruiter can provide you with detailed information on what that branch can offer currently in the following areas:

- available jobs (not every military job is available at a given time)
- education and training programs
- duty location
- enlistment program options, such as "Delayed Entry" and the "Buddy Program"
- enlistment qualification requirements

A recruiter will ask you some initial questions about your age, health history, and education. If you meet the basic requirements for that service branch, the recruiter will advance you to the next step: the Military Entrance Processing Station.

BEGINNING THE ENTRANCE PROCESS

About 60 Military Entrance Processing Stations—commonly called MEPS—dot the nation. People who have not already taken the ASVAB take the test at MEPS. There, recruits also receive a medical examination and meet with a military "classifier." A classifier is a career information specialist who will match your "aptitude" or career-potential with currently available military jobs. Just as in the civilian world, every job field doesn't always have openings. The classifier uses your ASVAB scores—both your AFQT and various subtest scores—to see whether you are qualified for various jobs. Again, that's why it's so important to prepare well for the test.

SIGNING ON THE DOTTED LINE

At the MEPS station, if you are found fit and qualified for military service, you'll be offered the opportunity to enlist immediately. If you do, you'll sign the dotted line on an enlistment contract and get on a bus or plane to head for basic training. Another option is "Delayed Entry Program" or DEP. Under DEP, you may return to MEPS at a scheduled date in the future and sign your official enlistment contract at that time. Some people choose DEP because the guaranteed military job training program they wanted was not available. They're hoping it will become available at a later time. Others enter DEP because they need to finish high school or take care of other personal obligations.

SO WHAT'S IN IT FOR YOU?

Some people who set out to join the armed forces don't hesitate at all before signing on the dotted line. What do they know that you don't? Maybe they've learned—through research or through an active-duty friend or relative—that military service offers big rewards. Below, we've sketched out the mountaintops—some of the really big advantages of joining the military.

EDUCATION

One of the first things you'll hear from a recruiter is how the military will pay for your college degree. That's a stone-cold fact. At this writing, the Montgomery G.I. Bill (MGIB) program provides military veterans with nearly $20,000, which can be used toward degree and certificate programs, flight training, apprenticeship/on-the-job training, and distance learning.

But you don't have to wait until you're a veteran (out of the service) to get financial help with your degree. Through a program called "Tuition Assistance," the military also will pay for up to 75% of all tuition costs while you're still on active duty. Every active-duty servicemember enjoys access to free education guidance counseling and base and post Education Offices (EO). And every service branch offers flexible degree programs. Such programs include "distance learning" (in which you earn your degree while studying on your own, off campus), and even college classes offered on your base or post.

ON-THE-JOB TRAINING

Every military servicemember is trained in a specific vocational or professional skill. Some jobs are technical, like those in computer technology or avionics. Others are administrative or trade positions. Whatever military job you choose, the military trains you *while you work and earn*. That training, combined with practical work experience, can give you an edge over civilian job applicants after you leave the service.

PERSONAL DEVELOPMENT

An Army television ad once said, "We do more before 9 A.M. than most people do all day." That's probably true of the military: It's more than just a job—it's a way of life. That's why serving in the armed forces can help you gain experiences and develop personal qualities that will help you in many areas of life. By traveling the world and meeting people from different cultures, military servicemembers learn to get along well with other people. By learning to get up early and work hard, soldiers, sailors, and airmen learn self-discipline and how a solid work ethic pays big rewards. Military service *changes* people—and changes them for the better. If you're looking for positive change, the armed forces may be the place you'll find it.

FINANCIAL BENEFITS

In addition to education, training, and personal benefits, the military also is a paying profession. Granted, the pay starts low at first. But remember: you're also an on-the-job trainee, earning while you learn. And while you're earning regular pay, you're also earning monetary allowances for food and housing. Once you ascend above the grade of E-5 (a sergeant in all services, except for the Navy and Coast Guard, where an E-5 is a Petty Officer Second Class), you can make a good living in the armed forces.

Besides a paycheck, the military also offers other financial benefits. While serving on active duty, comprehensive medical and dental care is available to servicemembers at no cost. It's also available to their immediate families at zero or very little cost. Should you retire from military service, your health coverage will continue at a cost substantially below that of civilian health care plans.

And speaking of retirement, many military servicemembers retire at the ripe old age of 38. That's right: Thousands of young people join the service at age 18, serve 20 years, and receive a military pension check every month for the rest of their lives. Meanwhile they've retired from the military so young that they've launched a *second* 20-year career, and earned a *second* lifelong pension. Not a bad way to wind up at age 58.

Education, job training, personal development, travel, financial benefits—not too many jobs offer those kinds of benefits. Below, learn how military service can help you, even after you've finished your enlistment.

POST-MILITARY CAREER OPTIONS

Thousands of employers have a positive view of work skills and habits gained during military service. Many also actively recruit veterans for the abilities they've acquired. Those qualities include, of course, the skills needed to do specific jobs. But they also include "soft skills"—like problem-solving ability and attention-to-detail—and other traits not related to a specific job. Below are a few reasons why company recruiters like job hunters with military experience:

Value-Added Skills

Military members often gain extra skills from part-time responsibilities like "Safety Coordinator" or "Training Officer." These duties help each military unit meet mission requirements, and are not always related to a servicemember's regular job. Employers in general are looking to get the most "bang for their buck." Part-time military duties add value to you as a job candidate, and can show hiring managers that you can handle extra responsibility.

Flexibility

In war, an enemy general rarely cooperates with his opponent's plans. That's why the military trains its members to be flexible, always ready to take on a new challenge. Many companies like job candidates who aren't afraid to tackle new assignments. They seek out veterans because they know they'll get a new hire who is flexible and enjoys new challenges.

Details, Details

Preparing and maintaining good records and files is a key part of many military jobs. Servicemembers who can perform those duties well are also attractive to civilian employers. In both the military and civilian worlds, being detail oriented makes you a valuable job candidate.

Leadership and Management

Servicemembers can often successfully market leadership and management skills. Many law enforcement agencies look specifically for supervisory experience combined with heavy doses of interpersonal skills.

Security Clearances

A current, high-level security clearance can be a big seller in the private sector, especially among government contract employers who work with classified military information and systems. Even servicemembers with a few transferable job skills may be able to land employment based almost entirely on a current clearance.

"Soft" Skills

Employers are equally, if not more, concerned about which candidate will be the best worker. Military members make attractive candidates because of their reputation for being punctual, working well with others and displaying a solid work ethic. Servicemembers are also known to be loyal and take initiative—traits that civilian employers also value highly.

To sum up, a service career not only can train you in a specific job that will last you the duration of your time in the military. It can also prepare you as a well-rounded job candidate for a successful future in the private sector.

But there's one gate you still must walk through in order to consider joining the military, and that's the ASVAB. You've seen from this chapter that this book will help you read more effectively. It will refresh your math skills and help you pick up a couple of new ones. This book will also help you learn to study and take tests like a pro. To top it all off, you'll learn to create a workable study plan that will help you achieve a high score on the ASVAB and AFQT.

Are you ready? Let's get started!

S·E·C·T·I·O·N 1

STUDYING FOR SUCCES

This section provides you with many helpful tips and advice to help you get ready for your test so that you feel in control and ready to score your best on the ASVAB. Taking the ASVAB is a challenge. If you want to achieve a top score, you must study hard to prepare. Your chances of getting into the service branch of your choice and getting the training you want depend on your performance on the exam, and there are all sorts of pitfalls that can keep you from doing your best on this all-important exam.

Here are some of the obstacles that can stand in the way of your success:

- being unfamiliar with the format of the exam
- not knowing what subtests are on the exam
- being paralyzed by test anxiety
- leaving your preparation to the last minute
- not preparing at all

What's the common denominator in all these test-taking pitfalls? One word: control. Who's in control, you or the exam? The first step toward taking control of your test experience is to learn everything you can about the ASVAB.

HISTORY OF THE ASVAB

For all intents and purposes, the U.S. military invented standardized testing, starting around the time of World War I. Then as now, the Department of Defense wanted to make sure that its recruits were trainable—not necessarily that they already had the skills they needed to serve in the armed forces, but that new recruits had the capability to learn them.

While the ASVAB started as a kind of intelligence test, now it is a test of specific aptitudes and abilities. Some of these aptitudes, such as reading and math problem-solving skills, are important for almost any job; others, such as electronics or automotive principles, are necessary for more specialized jobs.

TAKING THE EXAM

Try to start studying for the exam well in advance. Break your studying down into chunks so that you feel you can accomplish a set goal at each study session. This book is broken down into convenient chunks to help you accomplish specific goals with each lesson. Once you have studied the material, review it often.

Create a plan to get yourself through the material. Start with the most challenging material while you are still fresh. Then, move on to easier tasks as you tire.

Each time you go to study, do a quick review of your last lesson. This act will help your mind retain all you have learned. Each time you review the material, you will remember more than before. Reviewing is also a good way to assess how effectively you are studying: If you remember everything you learned the last time you studied, great; if not, try some of the studying techniques mentioned later in this section.

A week or more before your exam, take an hour or more to look over all the material you have studied. It can help you determine what material is most difficult for you, and in which areas you still need the most work.

It's important for you to realize that your score on the ASVAB, or its various subtests, does not determine what kind of person you are. There are all kinds of skills a written exam like this can't test—whether you can follow orders, whether you can become part of a unit that works together to accomplish a task, whether you will show courage under fire (if necessary), and so on. Although they are an important part of life in the military, those kinds of things are hard to evaluate and aren't tested on the ASVAB.

The ASVAB only covers qualities that can be evaluated on a standardized test. Despite the fact that even the strictest drill sergeant would agree that the test can't measure some fundamentally important personal characteristics, your chances of getting into the military and of getting the training you want still depend on your scores on certain portions of the ASVAB. And that's why you're here learning all you can—to achieve control over the exam.

Find out what kind of test taker you are by taking the quiz on the next page.

WHAT KIND OF TEST TAKER ARE YOU?

Check the sentences below that best describe your test-ability. As you think about your own experiences as a test taker, you'll find out more a little about the way you feel about tests.

_____ **1.** I am always nervous about tests.

_____ **2.** I am nervous about tests only when I don't feel confident about my performance.

_____ **3.** Sometimes the more I study, the worse I do on exams.

_____ **4.** If I have the time to study, I score better.

_____ **5.** I do best on tests when I cram for them.

_____ **6.** When I take a test, I want to know the results immediately.

_____ **7.** When I take a test, I don't want to know the results immediately.

_____ **8.** When I get nervous on tests, I freeze up.

_____ **9.** I do better on tests when I study alone.

_____ **10.** I do better on tests when I study with a friend.

_____ **11.** I study better when I am in a quiet room.

_____ **12.** I study better when I can hear the radio or television.

_____ **13.** Sometimes I am surprised when I get a lower score than I expected.

_____ **14.** I sometimes get a better score on a test than I expected.

_____ **15.** I sometimes study the wrong things for a test.

My worst experience with a test was when

_____

_____

_____

_____

_____

because

_____

_____

_____

_____

_____

My best experience with a test was when

_____

_____

_____

_____

because

_____

_____

_____

_____

Now that you have completed this evaluation, think about your answers and use what you've discovered to help you study and ace the ASVAB.

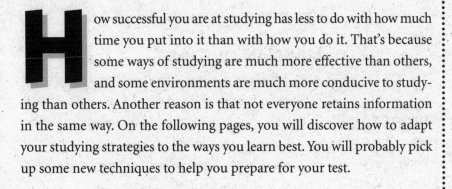

L·E·S·S·O·N
LEARNING STRATEGIES
1

How successful you are at studying has less to do with how much time you put into it than with how you do it. That's because some ways of studying are much more effective than others, and some environments are much more conducive to studying than others. Another reason is that not everyone retains information in the same way. On the following pages, you will discover how to adapt your studying strategies to the ways you learn best. You will probably pick up some new techniques to help you prepare for your test.

LEARNING STYLES

Think for a minute about what you know about how you learn. (Your answers on the "What Kind of Test Taker Are You" evaluation on pages 3 and 4 should help you.) You've lived long enough to have a good feel for how you learn what you need to learn. For example, if you need directions to a new restaurant would you:

- Ask to see a map showing how to get there?
- Ask someone to tell you how to get there?
- Copy someone's written directions?

Most people learn in a variety of ways: seeing, touching, hearing, and experiencing the world around them. Many people find, however, that they are more likely to absorb information from one learning source than from others. The source that works best for you is called your dominant learning method.

There are three basic learning methods: the visual, the auditory, and the kinesthetic (also known as tactile).

- Visual learners understand and retain information best when they can **see** the map, the picture, the text, the word, or the math example.
- Auditory learners learn best when they can **hear** the directions, the poem, the math theorem, or the spelling of a word.
- Kinesthetic learners need to **do**—they must write the directions, draw the diagram, or copy down the phone number.

VISUAL LEARNERS

If you are a visual learner, you learn best by seeing. Pay special attention to illustrations and graphic material when you study. If you color code your notes with colorful inks or highlighters, you may find that you absorb information better. Visual learners can learn to map or diagram information later in this chapter.

AUDITORY LEARNERS

If you are an auditory learner, you learn best by listening. Read material aloud to yourself, or talk about what you are learning with a study partner or a study group. Hearing the information will help you to remember it. Some people like to tape-record notes and play them back on the tape player. If you commute to work or school by car or listen to a personal tape player, you can gain extra preparation time by playing the notes to yourself on tape.

KINESTHETIC LEARNERS

If you are a kinesthetic learner, you learn best by doing. Interact a lot with your print material by underlining and making margin notes in your textbooks and handouts. Rewrite your notes onto index cards. Recopying material helps you to remember it.

HOW TO STUDY MOST EFFECTIVELY

If studying efficiently is second nature to you, you're very lucky. Most people have to work at it. Try some of these helpful study methods to make studying easier and more effective for you.

MAKE AN OUTLINE

After collecting all the materials you need to review or prepare for the test, the first step for studying any subject is to reduce a large body of information into smaller, more manageable units. One approach to studying this way is to make an outline of text information, handout material, and class notes.

The important information in print material is often surrounded by lots of extra words and ideas. If you can highlight just the important information, or at least the information you need to know for your test, you can help yourself narrow your focus so that you can study more effectively. There are several ways to make an outline of print material. They include annotating, outlining, and mapping. The point of all three of these strategies is that they allow you to pull out just the important information that you need to prepare for the test.

Annotating

Annotations help you pull out main ideas from the surrounding text to make them more visible and accessible to you. Annotation means that you underline or highlight important information that appears in print material. It also involves responding to the material by engaging yourself with the writer by making margin notes. Margin notes are phrases or sentences in the margins of print material that summarize the content of those passages. Your margin notes leave footprints for you to follow as you review the text.

Here is an example of a passage that has been annotated and underlined.

LOCATION, LOCATION, LOCATION

<u>Find a quiet spot, have a good reading light, and turn the radio off.</u>

Find Quiet Places

[margin note: Different quiet places at different times]

For many adult test takers, it's difficult to find a quiet spot in their busy lives. Many adults don't even have a bedroom corner that isn't shared with someone else. <u>Your quiet spot may be in a different place at different times of the day.</u>

For example, it could be the kitchen table early in the morning before breakfast, your workplace area when everyone else is at lunch, or a corner of the sofa late at night. If you know you'll have to move around when you study, <u>make sure your study material is portable.</u>

[margin note: Portable study material]

Keep your notes, practice tests, pencils, and other supplies together in a folder or bag. Then you can easily carry your study material with you and study in whatever quiet spot presents itself.

<u>If quiet study areas are non-existent in your home or work environment, you may need to find a space elsewhere. The public library is the most obvious choice.</u> Some test takers find it helpful to assign themselves study hours at the library in the same way that they schedule dentist appointments, class hours, household tasks, or other necessary uses of daily or weekly time. Studying away from home or job also minimizes the distractions of other people and other demands when you are preparing for a test.

[margin note: Library!]

Lights

[margin note: Need good light]

Libraries also provide good reading lights. For some people this may seem like a trivial matter, but the eyestrain that can come from working for long periods in <u>poor light can be very tiring—a cause of fatigue you can't afford when you're studying hard.</u>

At home, the bedside lamp, the semi-darkness of a room dominated by the television, or the bright sunlight of the back porch will be of little help to tired eyes.

Outlining

You are probably familiar with the basic format of the traditional outline:

I. Main idea 1
    A. Major detail
    B. Major detail
        1. Minor detail
        2. Minor detail
II. Main idea 2
    A. Major detail
    B. Major detail

You may have used an outline in school to help you organize a writing assignment or take notes. When you outline print material, you're looking for the basic ideas that make up the framework of the text. When you are taking out the important information for a test, then you are looking for the basic ideas that the author wants to convey to you.

Mapping

Mapping is a more visual kind of outline. Instead of a making a linear outline of the main ideas of a text, when you map, you make a diagram of the main points in the text that you want to remember. The following diagrams shows the same information in a map form.

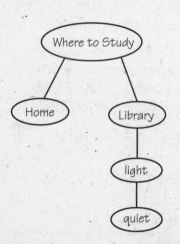

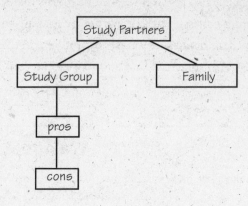

MAKE STUDY NOTES

The next step after you have pulled out all the key ideas is to make notes from which you will study. You will use these notes for the intensive and ongoing study you'll do over the period of time before the test. They're the specific items that you targeted as important to know for the test. Your notes should help you understand the information you need to know and, in many cases, commit it to memory. You should be sure to include:

- the main ideas you underlined or highlighted in the text
- the main ideas and important details you outlined or mapped from the text
- specific terms, words, dates, formulas, names, facts, or procedures that you need to memorize

How Do You Make Study Notes?

Some people like to write study notes in the back pages of their notebooks or on paper folded lengthwise so that it can be tucked between the pages of a text or review book. This format is good to use for notes that can be written as questions and answers, cause and effect, or definition and examples. You can also make notes on index cards.

Using Index Cards

It can be very helpful to write your study notes—especially those that contain material to be memorized—on index cards.

The advantages of making notes on index cards are:

- The information on each card is visually separated from other information. Therefore it's easier to concentrate on just that one item, separate from the surrounding text. You remember the look of a vocabulary word or a math equation more clearly when it is set off by itself.
- Cards are small and portable. They can be carried in a purse or a pocket and pulled out at any time during the day for review.
- Study cards can help you with the necessary task of memorizing. If you write the key word or topic you are trying to learn on one side, and the information you must know on the other side, you have an easy wasy to quiz yourself on the material. This method is especially good for kinesthetic learners, who learn by doing.

MAKING MEMORIZING EASIER

There are many ways to take the drudgery out of memorizing information.

TAKE SMALL BITES OF TIME

Most people memorize information best when they study in small periods over a long period of time.

Memorizing facts from index cards that can be carried with you and pulled out for a few ten-minute sessions each day will yield better results than sitting down with a textbook for an hour straight. Index card notes can be pulled out in odd moments: while you are sitting in the car waiting to pick up your friend, the quiet fifteen minutes you spend on the bus in the morning, while you wait to be picked up from school or work, and so on.

You'll find that these short but regular practices will greatly aid your recall of lots of information. They're a great way to add more study time to your schedule.

BREAK IT UP

When you have a list to memorize, break the list into groups of seven or any other odd number. People seem to remember best when they divide long lists into shorter ones—and, for some reason, shorter ones that have an odd number of items in them. So instead of trying to memorize ten vocabulary or spelling words, split your list into smaller lists of seven and three, or five and five, to help you remember them.

CREATE VISUAL AIDS

Give yourself visual assistance in memorizing. If there's a tricky combination of letters in a word you need to spell, for example, circle or underline it in red or highlight it in the text. Your eye will recall what the word looks like. With some information, you can even draw a map or picture to help you remember.

DO IT OUT LOUD

Give yourself auditory assistance in memorizing. Many people learn best if they *hear* the information. Sit by yourself in a quiet room and say aloud what you need to learn. Or, give your notes to someone else and let that person ask you or quiz you on the material.

USE MNEMONICS

Mnemonics, or memory tricks, are things that help you remember what you need to know.

The most common type of mnemonic is the acronym (a word created from the first letters in a series of words). One acronym you may already know is HOMES, for the names of the Great Lakes (Huron, Ontario, Michigan, Erie, and Superior). ROY G BIV reminds people of the colors in the spectrum (Red, Orange, Yellow, Green, Blue, Indigo, and Violet).

You can make a mnemonic out of anything. In a psychology course, for example, you might memorize the stages in death and dying by the nonsense word DABDA (denial, anger, bargaining, depression, and acceptance.) Another kind of mnemonic is a silly sentence made out of words that each begin with the letter or letters that start each item in a series. You may remember "Please Excuse My Dear Aunt Sally" as a device for remembering the order of operations in math (parentheses, exponents, multiply, divide, add, and subtract).

SLEEP ON IT

When you study right before sleep and don't allow any interference—such as conversation, radio, television, or music—to come between study and sleep, you remember material better. This is especially true if you review first thing after waking as well. A rested and relaxed brain seems to hang on to information better than a tired and stressed-out brain.

On the following pages, try out some of the learning strategies you discovered in this lesson. Then, check your answers.

Below is a passage from this text to underline and annotate. Make margin summaries of the key points in each paragraph. Then make a mnemonic based on your margin notes.

Take Small Bites of Time

Most people memorize information best when they study in small periods over a long period of time.

Memorizing facts from index cards that can be carried with you and pulled out for a few ten-minute sessions each day will yield better results than sitting down with a textbook for an hour straight. You'll find that these short but regular practices will greatly aid your recall of lots of information. They're a great way to add more study time to your schedule.

Break It Up

When you have a list to memorize, break the list into groups of seven or any other odd number. People seem to remember best when they divide long lists into shorter ones—and, for some reason, shorter ones that have an odd number of items in them. So instead of trying to memorize ten vocabulary or spelling words, split your list into smaller lists of seven and three, or five and five, to help you remember them.

Create Visual Aids

Give yourself visual assistance in memorizing. If there's a tricky combination of letters in a word you need to spell, for example, circle or underline it in red or highlight it in the text. Your eye will recall what the word looks like.

Do It Out Loud

Give yourself auditory assistance in memorizing. Many people learn best if they hear the information. Sit by yourself in a quiet room and say aloud what you need to learn. Or, give your notes to someone else and let that person ask you questions and quiz you on the material.

Use Mnemonics

Mnemonics, or memory tricks, are things that help you remember what you need to know.

The most common type of mnemonic is the acronym (a word created from the first letters in a series of words). One acronym you may already know is HOMES, for the names of the Great Lakes (Huron, Ontario, Michigan, Erie, and Superior). ROY G BIV reminds people of the colors in the spectrum (Red, Orange, Yellow, Green, Blue, Indigo, and Violet).

Note Cards

Make note cards with definitions for each kind of learning modality:

- visual
- auditory
- kinesthetic

Mapping

Below is an outline of the learning strategies covered in this chapter. Using the same information, make a map, or diagram, of the same material.

I. How to study most effectively

    A. Annotating

    B. Outlining

    C. Mapping

II. How to make study notes

    A. Notebook pages

    B. Index cards

        1. Reasons for using index cards

III. Memory methods

COMPLETED SAMPLE
ANNOTATION

Take Small Bites of Time

Distributed practice

Most people memorize information best when they study in <u>small periods over a long period of time.</u>

Memorizing facts from portable index cards that can be carried with you and pulled out for a few ten-minute sessions each day will yield better results than sitting down with a text-book for an hour straight. You'll find that these short but regular practices will greatly aid your recall of lots of information. They're a great way to add more study time to your schedule.

Break It Up

Divide lists

When you have a list to memorize, <u>break the list into groups of seven or any other odd number.</u> People seem to remember best when they divide long lists into shorter ones—and, for some reason, shorter ones that have an odd number of items in them. So instead of trying to memorize ten vocabulary or spelling words, split your list into smaller lists of seven and three, or five and five, to help you remember them.

Create Visual Aids

Visual Aids

<u>Give yourself visual assistance in memorizing.</u> If there's a tricky combination of letters in a word you need to spell, for example, circle or underline it in red or highlight it in the text. Your eye will recall what the word looks like.

Do It Out Loud

Auditory

<u>Give yourself auditory assistance in memorizing.</u> Many people learn best if they hear the information. Sit by yourself in a quiet room and say aloud what you need to learn. Or, give your notes to someone else and let that person ask you questions and quiz you on the material.

Use Mnemonics

<u>Mnemonics</u>, or memory tricks, are things that help you remember what you need to know.

Acronym

The most common type of mnemonic is the <u>acronym</u> (a word created from the first let-ters in a series of words). One acronym you may already know is HOMES, for the names of the Great Lakes (Huron, Ontario, Michigan, Erie, and Superior). ROY G BIV reminds peo-ple of the colors in the spectrum (Red, Orange, Yellow, Green, Blue, Indigo, and Violet).

Sample Mnemonic
DDVAA

Note Cards
Here are samples of how your note cards might look:

Visual Modality	Auditory Modality	Kinesthetic Modality
learning by seeing	learning by listening	learning by doing

Mapping
Here is an example of how your map or diagram might look:

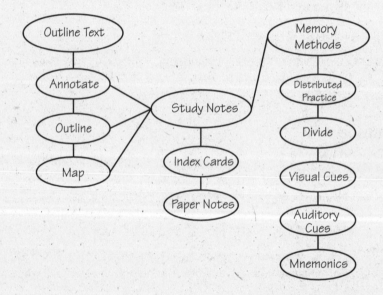

L·E·S·S·O·N

YOUR STUDY PLAN

Preparing for a test is most effective if you have a system that keeps you focused on a very specific goal. And your goal in this case is to get the very best score possible on your ASVAB. As in most things in life, the more you plan to succeed, the more often you will succeed. And remember, your true goal is not just to scrape by on a test; it's to do well on the test.

This lesson will guide you, step-by-step, through the process of setting up a study plan for the ASVAB. Contact your recruiter or guidance counselor who can tell you when you will take the exam. Then, once you know when you will take the ASVAB, you need to create a study plan to schedule your time leading up to a test. After you establish how much time you have to prepare for the test, gather all your test materials and review books to help you establish your specific plan.

STEP 1: SET A TIME FRAME

Don't fall into the cram trap. Take control of your preparation time by mapping out a long-term study schedule; you can't improve the skills the ASVAB is testing for overnight. You have to set aside some time every day for study and practice. Try for at least 30 minutes a day.

STEP 2: GET THE CORRECT INFORMATION

Check your testing kit and talk to your recruiter. Read the directions and suggestions for success that come with any papers about the ASVAB you receive from your recruiter or guidance counselor.

STEP 3: GET ALL YOUR MATERIALS TOGETHER

Look over all your review materials carefully to be sure you understand everything. If you don't, try comparing notes with others you know who are taking the ASVAB, or an adult who is knowledgeable about reading, math, and vocabulary skills. Finish any sections you may have missed. Check to make sure you have completed all practice problems and exercises.

STEP 4: STAY ON YOUR PLAN AND REWARD YOURSELF FOR GOOD BEHAVIOR

Treat yourself to an afternoon walk, a candy bar, a long phone chat with a friend—anything that will reward you for maintaining a good study schedule. It isn't easy, and you should pat yourself on the back when you can stick to your routine for some period of time.

SAMPLE STUDY PLAN

Because each type of test is different, each should have its own study plan. Here is an example to get you started thinking about what *you* will need for your study plan. Remember, the hardest part about making a plan

is actually starting the plan. Make a promise to yourself right now to start your plan and continue with it so that you can do your best on the ASVAB.

When you meet with your recruiter or guidance counselor you should:

1. **Request all materials needed for the test.** Your recruiter or guidance counselor should give you a packet of information about the test.
2. **Find out your test date.** After your meeting, buy a desk or wall calendar and enter the date of your test so that you can visualize an end study goal to shoot for.
3. **Find more review material.** Browse bookstores or libraries for other review material that contains sample tests. Buy or borrow one or two that seem appropriate. LearningExpress offers practice tests for the ASVAB both in print (*ASVAB*: LearningExpress: 2001; *ASVAB Core Review.* LearningExpress: 1998) and online (visit www.learnatest.com). Make a note of all resources available to you in case you feel you need more practice later.
4. **Figure out the format of the test.** You should now have enough information about the ASVAB to analyze the format of the test. You should know how many questions are in each section and how long the test takes.
5. **Take a couple of sample tests from a review book and check your scores.** See how you performed on each part of the test to help you gauge which areas you may need to improve and in which areas your skills are strong.
6. **Study more in each of your weakest areas.** Take more practice tests. The strategies you are learning in this book should help you complete these practice tests more successfully. Set aside

at least one hour a day to review the all areas you want to improve.

7. **Continue to review for half an hour to an hour five days a week.** Notice that, contrary to expectations, you are spending fewer hours a week in preparation. If you have been reviewing regularly, the reviews should take you less time since you're so accustomed to the questions. This is the most important part of preparing for tests. The more familiar you are with the test, the better you will perform under testing conditions.

Just before the test:

1. **Confirm the date of the test.** Make sure you know where the test will be held and how you will get to the test site.
2. **Spend more time reviewing.** Note how much your scores have improved since you began your review.
3. **Concentrate on being well rested and relaxed about the test.**

The night before the test:

Get organized. Make sure that you have everything you need ready to take with you to the exam and that you have arranged for plenty of time to get to the test site.

With an important test, it's just too risky to rely on luck alone. Staying casual about your exam, playing the procrastination game, and only dabbling with a study plan could very well mean sabotaging your chances of success. The better you plan out your time before you take the ASVAB, the more comfortable you will be on test day.

YOUR OWN STUDY PLAN

In the space below, write in a schedule for the time prior to taking the ASVAB.

The test I need to take is

_____

It will be held on

_____

The test site is located at

_____

Three questions I have about the test are

_____

_____

_____

I plan to study for this test as follows:
One month before the test

_____

_____

_____

Two weeks before the test

_____

_____

One week before the test

_____

_____

Two days before the test

_____

_____

_____

The day before the test

_____

_____

_____

TIME MANAGEMENT

You have already set up a basic time frame by making your plan; however, you still need to figure out how you are going to use the time up until the test most effectively. All the plans in the world won't help you if you don't find time to actually study what you need to know to pass the test. You have to find the time to put your plan into action.

MAKING YOUR PLAN FIT YOU

Here are some strategies for testing your plan against what you know about your personal time patterns and commitments:

1. **Figure out what time you have available to study in a typical week.** Write down what you do on one typical work or school day and one typical weekend day.
2. **Notice what hours seem to be free for study.** Are most of those hours in the evenings? In the daytime? How many hours do you have available for study? Is your study time in blocks? (All Wednesday afternoons and Saturday mornings, for example.) Or is your study time in bits and pieces during the week? (An hour each morning and half an hour late in the afternoon before the bus comes.)
3. **Determine your own patterns of rest and fatigue.** Are you a morning person who can get up an hour early and study before breakfast? Are you a night owl who can work after everyone else is asleep? Are you accustomed to exercising regularly? Does exercise tire or energize you?

Answering these questions will help you to choose the times that are best for you to study. Once you've answered the questions, consider how your time frame fits the study plan you've devised.

ANTICIPATE TIME CONFLICTS

If you have to take the ASVAB in late November right after your Thanksgiving weekend at Aunt Dot's, or the test is just two days after you get back from vacation to Chicago, the timing's not good, but at least you know in advance and can plan accordingly. You can do most of your studying before you leave town. It's inevitable that you will encounter conflicts—life goes on, test or no test. Accept the fact that many things are going to come up at home or at work over which you have no control. Learn to handle your time so that things that come up won't get in the way of your study plan.

ALWAYS FACTOR IN EXTRA TIME

If a test is going to be given on the 12th, mark the 10th as the date you want to be ready for the test. Whenever possible, build in a few days of extra time to prepare for a test. These extra days will be your insurance policy in case you get sick, have a work or family crisis, or encounter another difficulty that limits your study time and jeopardizes your success on a test. In addition, be sure to study where you study best. For example, work as much as possible in the library where distractions will be at a minimum.

WHEN TIME IS RUNNING OUT

The test date is looming and you're beginning to get tense. Despite your planning, you find yourself faced with just too little time to do what needs to be done to really be prepared. When you have less time than you would like to prepare for one big test, you have to decide which part of the study plan needs the most immediate attention and the largest commitment of your time—in other words, you must prioritize. Figure out what areas you need to study the most and what areas can you skim.

STICKING TO YOUR PLAN

Now that you have a plan that will work, here are some strategies for sticking to it:

- **Write down your study schedule.** Post a copy where it will remind you of the times you need to study.
- **Don't abandon your study plan if you get off track for a few days.** It's easy to become discouraged when outside events, work, school obligations, family responsibilities, or

personal problems keep you from your studies during the time you have scheduled for studying. Just pick up where you left off. Try to add a little time to two or three study sessions rather than trying to make up for lost study time by cramming, or by skipping important material.

- **Adjust your study plan to meet changing needs.** For example, if you find that you need to do more practice tests than you had planned to do, take more time to do them. If you find that you are doing well on specific sections and less well on others, take more time on those sections that need your attention.

You can create your own Weekly Timetable on the next page. It will give you a place to incorporate all your responsibilities, including study time. If you're not sure what to include, you can also take a look at the completed sample, on the following page.

WEEKLY TIMETABLE

On the timetable for a week below, cross out any hours when you are occupied with work, school, family, recreation, meals, and any activities you do on a regular basis—team sports, community work, volunteer work, and so on. See what hours you have free to study.

	Sunday	Monday	Tuesday	Wednesday	Thursday	Friday	Saturday
6:00							
7:00							
8:00							
9:00							
10:00							
11:00							
12:00							
1:00							
2:00							
3:00							
4:00							
5:00							
6:00							
7:00							
8:00							
9:00							
10:00							
11:00							
12:00							

WEEKLY TIMETABLE

Completed

	Sunday	Monday	Tuesday	Wednesday	Thursday	Friday	Saturday
6:00							
7:00							
8:00							
9:00		✕	✕	✕	✕	✕	
10:00	✕	✕	✕	✕	✕	✕	
11:00	✕	✕	✕	✕	✕	✕	✕
12:00	←		LUNCH			→	✕ *ERRANDS*
1:00		✕	✕	✕	✕	✕	✕
2:00		✕	✕	✕	✕	✕	✕
3:00		✕	✕	✕	✕	✕	
4:00		✕	✕	✕	✕	✕	
5:00	✕		DINNER		✕	✕	
6:00	✕	✕			✕	✕	
7:00	✕					✕	✕ *RECREATION*
8:00			✕ *BOWLING*	✕ *MEETING*			✕
9:00				✕			✕
10:00							
11:00							
12:00							

MANAGING TEST DAY

These strategies should help you sail through test day with hardly any stress.

LEAVE PLENTY OF TIME FOR YOURSELF

Even if your test is early in the morning, be sure that you have more than enough time to be settled before the test. This may take some extra planning.

- **Get up early.** Set two alarm clocks to be sure that you don't oversleep. If you are a heavy sleeper, ask someone to rouse you personally or to call your house to make sure you are awake.
- **Double-check the location and time of the test.** Write it down where you can see it, so the information doesn't get misplaced.
- **Get as much ready the night before as you can.** Have your clothing ready to jump into if necessary. Make sure there is gas in the car or get your public transportation fare ready the night before the test.
- **Know exactly where you're going and know the most reliable route for getting to the test site.** You will most likely be the guest of the Department of Defense in your trip to the Military Entrance Processing Center (MEPS). Your recruiter will tell you when and where you will be picked up for your trip to the MEPS. Make sure you know how to get to that location—if it's not your recruiting station—and how long it will take to get there. Figure out how early you'll have to get up that morning, and get up that early every day for a week before your MEPS day.

FEEL GOOD

To do a good job on the test, you have to feel good, both mentally and physically.

- **Stay healthy.** Be especially careful of your health near exam time; stay away from people who have been sick. If you must tend a sick child or family member, do your best to keep germs at bay by taking some simple precautions like washing your hands frequently and keeping food and drink utensils separate.
- **Sleep well.** The night before a test is not a good night to stay out late or overindulge in food or drink. The morning after these activities is not a good morning to take a test.
- **Dress comfortably.** Dress in layers; you don't know what the temperature of the testing room may be. At any time of the year the room could be ice cold or stifling hot. If you wear a sweater, you can take it off if it's stuffy or put it on if it's chilly.
- **Eat lightly, but nutritionally.** A heavy meal before a test may make you sleepy or sluggish. A breakfast of cereal, fruit, or yogurt, or a simple sandwich and soup for lunch before a test, will make you feel fueled, but not uncomfortably full.
- **Exercise moderately.** If exercise relaxes or energizes you, build in time for your morning run or brisk walk before leaving for the test. Mild exercise can be very helpful in relieving stress and contributing to feelings of well being. You should refrain from a strenuous workout so you won't tire yourself before the exam.
- **Don't drink too much.** If the test is a long test, don't drink a lot of coffee or soda before

the test. Most tests won't have bathroom breaks.

- **Think positively.** Positive thoughts about your preparation for the test will contribute to your success—if you are not too stressed out about the exam, you will be able to concentrate fully on the subject at hand and do your best.

MAKE SURE YOU HAVE THE SUPPLIES YOU NEED

Remember to take sharp #2 pencils with you, if you need them—and anything else you might need during the test.

- **Take admissions materials.** If there are admission cards or documents you must take to the exam, be sure you have them ready and handy on the morning of the test.
- **Limit your study materials.** Take the minimum of study cards or notes with you. Don't carry your texts or review books to the testing site. You will be tempted to look at them and panic when you can't remember something that you run across in the text. By the time you are ready to take the test, your notes should be boiled down to just the few you want to review very briefly right before the exam.
- **Wear a watch.** Make sure it is working.
- **Take a pack of tissues.** You can't think when your nose is running.
- **Take good luck with you.** If you are so inclined, put your lucky charm, rabbit's foot, or other comfort item in your pocket or bag.

WITH THE TEST IN FRONT OF YOU

Though you may be very anxious to get started on the test, resist the temptation to start working before all

instructions have been given. Pay particular attention to such things as:

- **How to fill out the answer sheets.** You may have a seat number or testing number that needs to be included or other personal data that is required on the test.
- **Time limits.** You need to know how long you have for each section of the test and whether there will be a break.
- **Keep moving.** Don't waste time on one question. If you don't know the answer, or how to figure it out, skip the question and move on. Circle the number of the question in your test booklet in case you have time to come back to it later.
- **Keep track of your place on the answer sheet.** If you skip a question, make sure you skip it on the answer sheet too. Check yourself every 5–10 questions to make sure the question number and the answer sheet number match up.
- **Don't rush.** Though you should keep moving, rushing won't help. Try to remain calm and work methodically and quickly.
- **Be confident.** When you first look at the test, take a deep breath and approach it with a take-charge attitude.

Exam day can be stressful, but using the techniques listed in this chapter, you can cut down on stress. When the big day finally arrives, you'll be ready to face it in an organized and systematic way.

L·E·S·S·O·N 3
THE MULTIPLE-CHOICE TEST

In this chapter you will learn how to deal with the multiple-choice test. This chapter introduces the multiple-choice format and deals with questions requiring recall or recognition of material.

All multiple-choice test questions are geared to tap into your knowledge of a subject or to measure your skills at performing some task. Some test questions require you to recall specific items of information, while others ask you only to recognize information by separating it from similar choices. Others have you reason out answers based on ideas presented in the test itself.

Generally speaking, multiple-choice questions are considered to be objective questions because they are fact-based; they don't allow for the opinion or interpretation of the test taker.

WHY MULTIPLE-CHOICE?

Like most short answer tests, multiple-choice tests are easier and quicker to grade. Furthermore, they do not penalize test takers who know the information but have poorly developed writing skills or problems with expressive language.

How the Questions are Written

You may remember taking tests that contained questions like this one:

1. The largest of the Great Lakes is
a. Huron.
b. Superior.
c. Erie.
d. Mississippi.

The question contains the three elements of most multiple-choice questions, which are stems, options, and distracters.

Stem: "The largest of the Great Lakes is"
Options: All answer choices
Distracters: Incorrect answer choices

STEMS

Stems contain the core information on which the question is based. In some tests, the stems of the questions may be as long as a paragraph and could contain a lot of information that you must sift through before you can choose an answer. Sometimes stem questions are phrased as situations. Situation questions set a scene or set of facts on which the test taker is required to answer a series of questions.

Stems can also be simply a word, a math example, or a fragment of a sentence that serves to frame the question.

OPTIONS

Options are the answer choices offered to you, the test taker. Many options require that you simply recognize a correct choice among several others.

2. As President, Ronald Reagan came to be known as
a. Old Hickory.
b. The Great Communicator.
c. Speaker of the House.
d. Old Ironsides.

The answer is *b*.

The question is trying to test the accuracy of your knowledge by offering two or more options that are similar.

3. The word in the following sentence that means the same or almost the same as flammable is
a. fireproof.
b. fire resistant.
c. easily burned.
d. burning.

It wouldn't be enough in this question that you know that flammable has something to do with fire. All of the options offer that choice. You have to know that the particular word pertaining to fire that you want means that something is easily burned, answer *c*.

DISTRACTERS

Distracters are the incorrect answers that offer a challenge to the test takers. In question 2, above, the distracters are *a*, *c*, and *d*; and in question 3, they are *a*, *b*, and *d*.

Distracters are often written to force test takers to be very careful in their selections. In question 2, for instance, if you didn't know that Reagan was known by the epithet The Great Communicator, you could be distracted by the two choices that refer to age. Since Reagan was one of our oldest presidents while in office, you might be tempted to choose one of them.

The wise test taker will eliminate the clearly impossible options first. In question 2, both Old Ironsides, which is the name of a ship, and Speaker of the House, which is an office that cannot be held by a sitting president, should be eliminated. Then, between Old Hickory and The Great Communicator, you would have to make a choice. If you remembered that Old Hickory was the term used to describe President Andrew Jackson, you would eliminate it, and then the correct choice would be obvious.

RECOGNITION AND RECALL QUESTIONS

As noted before, multiple-choice questions force you to recall or recognize specific information that is surrounded by other similar but incorrect options. These other options can be written in such a way that they confuse the unwary or unwise test taker.

4. Choose the word or phrase that means the same or almost the same as the word secession.
   a. a meeting
   b. the act of breaking away from a political body
   c. a surgical birth
   d. a parade

5. Circle the word that is correctly spelled in the following group of words.
   a. chanel
   b. channel
   c. chanle
   d. chanell

6. Choose the correct punctuation for the following sentence from the choices below: I went to lunch with my two
   a. sister in laws.
   b. sister-in-laws.
   c. sister's in law.
   d. sisters-in-law.

In questions 4–6, you would have to rely on your memory for the definition of secession, the spelling of the word channel, and the plural forms for hyphenated words, or you would have to be able to recognize the correct answer in comparison to the other choices. The correct answers are: 4 is *b*, 5 is *b*, and 6 is *d*. Some strategies for approaching these kinds of questions are outlined below.

Note distracters *c* and *d* in question 4. Many multiple-choice questions are designed to confuse you by offering options that sound like the stem word or have associations with the stem word. In this instance the similarity between procession and secession, and the distant but confusing sound similarities between secession and the medical short hand C-section for cesarean section could trap the unwary test taker.

- **Let Your Eye Be Your Guide.** Look at the four choices of spelling. Which choice looks like something you've seen before? Choice *b*, channel.
- **Let Your Ear Be Your Guide.** Listen to the differences between sister-in-laws and sisters-in-law. Which sounds better? Sisters-in-law sounds better; plus, you know that there are two people involved, which would have to make your answer plural.
- **Try Each Option as a True/False Question.** "A secession is a meeting. True or false?" "A secession is an act of breaking away from a

political body. True or false?" Which statement seems to make the most sense?

READING QUESTIONS

Some multiple-choice questions are geared to measure your ability to take information directly from the text and to answer questions based on that text. These kinds of multiple-choice questions typically measure reading comprehension—you'll see them mostly in the Paragraph Comprehension subtest.

Generally, reading comprehension tests start with a passage on a particular subject, followed by as few as two or as many as ten questions based on the content of that passage.

These questions usually are aimed at four skills:

1. recognizing the definition of a vocabulary word in the passage
2. identifying the main idea of the passage
3. noting a specific fact or detail in the passage
4. making an inference or conclusion based on information in the passage that is not directly stated

Read the following passage and the four questions that follow. Identify each type of question from the list above.

The "broken window" theory was originally developed to explain how minor acts of vandalism or disrespect can quickly escalate to crimes and attitudes that break down the entire social fabric of an area or unit. It is an idea that can easily be applied to any situation in society. The theory contends that if a broken window in an abandoned building is not replaced quickly, soon all the windows in that building will be broken.

In other words, a small violation, if condoned, leads others to commit similar or greater violations. Thus, after all the windows have been broken, the building is likely to be looted and perhaps even burned down. According to this theory, violations increase exponentially. Thus, if disrespect to a superior is tolerated, others will be tempted to be disrespectful as well. A management crisis could erupt literally overnight.

For example, if one firefighter begins to disregard proper housewatch procedure by neglecting to keep up the housewatch administrative journal, and this firefighter is not reprimanded, others will follow suit by committing similar violations of procedure, thinking, "If he can get away with it, why can't I?" So what starts out as a small violation that may seem not to warrant disciplinary action, may actually ruin the efficiency of the entire firehouse, risking the lives of the people the firehouse serves.

7. In this passage the word "reprimanded" means
   a. scolded
   b. praised
   c. rewarded
   d. fired
Question type_____

8. The best title for this passage would be
   a. Broken Windows: Only the First Step
   b. The Importance of Housewatch
   c. How to Write an Administrative Journal
   d. A Guide to Window Repair
Question type_____

9. The passage suggests that
   a. firefighters are sloppy administrators.
   b. firefighters will blame others for mistakes.
   c. discipline starts with small infractions.
   d. discipline is important for the efficiency of the firehouse.
Question type_____

10. According to the passage, which of the following could be the result of broken windows?
    a. The building would soon be vandalized.
    b. Firefighters would lose morale.
    c. There could be a management crisis.
    d. The efficiency of the firehouse could be destroyed.

Question type_____

Answers

7. a. Reprimanded means scolded. (Vocabulary)

8. a. The passage is about the "broken window" theory, showing that a minor violation or breach of discipline can lead to major violations. (Main idea)

9. d. The passage applies the broken window theory to firehouse discipline, showing that even small infractions have to be dealt with to avoid worse problems later. (Inference)

10. a. See the third sentence of the passage. (Detail)

ANSWERING STRATEGIES

Answering many multiple-choice questions correctly requires either direct knowledge or recognition and recall of specific facts, or the ability to understand written information well enough to answer questions based on that written information.

A successful test taker will approach multiple-choice questions with several good strategies. They include:

1. **Always circle or underline the keywords in the stem that direct your search for the answer.** In the earlier examples, President was the keyword in question 2, and the same or almost the same were the keywords in question 4.

2. **Immediately eliminate all clearly incorrect distracters.** This will usually mean that you have to choose between two similar choices.

3. **Carefully read each question.** Beware of examiners' tricks to confuse you: look-alike options, easily confused options, and silly options. Watch for tricky wording such as "All of the following are true except . . ."

4. **Understand exactly what is being asked.** You will find distracters that are accurate and may sound right but do not apply to the stem.

5. **Beware of the absolute.** Read carefully any stem that includes words like always, never, none, or all. An answer may sound perfectly correct and the general principal may be correct. However, it may not be true in all circumstances. For example, think about the statement "All roses are red." *All* roses?

6. **Do the easiest questions first.** Many tests are arranged so that the questions move from easy to more difficult. Don't lose out on easier points by skipping over those early questions and risk running out of time.

On the following page, write one of each of the question types discussed in this chapter. If you can write one, you can answer one!

TRY OUT YOUR MULTIPLE-CHOICE QUESTION SKILLS

Read the following passage. Then write one of each of the four types of multiple-choice questions, based on the content of the passage.

Detectives who routinely investigate violent crimes can't help but become somewhat jaded.

Paradoxically, the victims and witnesses with whom they closely work are often in a highly vulnerable and emotional state. The emotional fallout from a sexual assault, for example, can be complex and long lasting. Detectives must be trained to handle people in emotional distress and must be sensitive to the fact that for the victim the crime is not routine. At the same time, detectives must recognize the limits of their role and resist the temptation to act as therapists or social workers instead of referring victims to the proper agencies.

1. A main idea question

_____

_____

a. _____

b. _____

c. _____

d. _____

2. A detail question

_____

_____

a. _____

b. _____

c. _____

d. _____

3. A vocabulary question

_____

_____

a. _____

b. _____

c. _____

d. _____

4. An inference question

_____

_____

a. _____

b. _____

c. _____

d. _____

TRY OUT YOUR MULTIPLE-CHOICE QUESTION SKILLS
(Sample answers)

1. A main idea question
What is the main idea of the passage?
   a. Detectives who investigate violent crime must never become emotionally hardened by the experience.
   b. Victims of violent crime should be referred to therapists and social workers.
   c. Detectives should be sensitive to the emotional state of victims of violent crime.
   d. Detectives should be particularly careful in dealing with victims of sexual assault.

2. A detail question
Which of the following would be an appropriate response by a detective to a victim in emotional distress?
   a. immediate assistance
   b. a sympathetic ear
   c. arrest of the perpetrator
   d. referral to social service agencies

3. A vocabulary question

In this passage, the word "jaded" means

a. nervous

b. lazy

c. insensitive

d. hostile

4. An inference question

The passage suggests that police detectives

a. are often arrogant in dealing with victims.

b. should be sympathetic to victims.

c. have responsibilities beyond the arrest of criminals.

d. are underpaid.

MATH QUESTIONS

Math questions on the ASVAB assess how a person applies basic math skills to workplace situations.

Some questions are mostly numerical in format:

1. What is the reciprocal of $3\frac{7}{8}$?

a. $\frac{31}{28}$

b. $\frac{8}{31}$

c. $\frac{8}{21}$

d. $\frac{31}{8}$

Some questions are introduced by stems in which the needed numerical information is embedded. In other words, they are word problems.

2. A city worker is paid time-and-a-half an hour in overtime pay. He earns $20 per hour. If he works four hours more than his contracted work week, how much does he make in overtime pay?

a. 80.00

b. 120.00

c. 400.00

d. 60.00

Answers

1. **b.** $3\frac{7}{8} = \frac{31}{8}$, whose reciprocal is $\frac{8}{31}$.

2. **b.** The worker makes $20 \times 1\frac{1}{2} = \$30$ per hour in overtime. Now multiply the hourly overtime wage by the number of overtime hours: $30 \times 4 = 120$.

STRATEGIES FOR ANSWERING MATH QUESTIONS

Even though you're dealing with numbers and not words in math questions, the way you analyze the questions and consider the possible answers is very similar to the types of word questions you read about earlier in the chapter.

- **Don't panic because it's math.** They're only numbers after all.
- **Read the stem carefully.** Underline or circle the most important information in the stem.
- **Read all the options carefully.** Don't be confused by distracting answer choices.
- **Work through the problem.** If you immediately see an answer that matches, you can move right on. Do all calculations on paper, not in your head.
- **Skip unfamiliar or difficult questions on the first pass through the test.** Put a dot in the margin of the test or circle the questions

so that you can locate the question quickly and easily if you are in a hurry.

- **Be careful when you write your calculations.** The number 1 can look like 7, 3 like 8, and 6 like 0 when you are in a hurry. If you don't take your time and write carefully, you risk picking up a wrong answer or wasting time recalculating an answer to find something that fits from your choice of answers.

- **Translate numbers from math into English.** *Reciprocal* in question 1 means the inverse of the fractional number. Take some time to translate words from English into math. Time and a half in question 2 means $1\frac{1}{2}$ or $\frac{3}{2}$.

SHOULD YOU GUESS?

The ASVAB doesn't penalize you for guessing. The number of questions you answer correctly yields your raw score. So you have nothing to lose and everything to gain by guessing. Even if you're really unsure of the answer you're still safe in guessing every time. Try to overcome your anxiety and go ahead and mark an answer.

As you know, multiple-choice questions usually have four or five options, only one of which is right. Theoretically, each answer gives you a 20–25% chance of being correct. If you raise the odds by eliminating one or more of those distracters right away, you are in an even better position to make a good guess. The problem is, what to do when you have two answers that sound equally correct?

USE THE TRUE/FALSE TEST

Try submitting the stem and each of the two options you are using to a true/false test.

1. The primary responsibility of the office manager is to
   a. get the CEO's coffee promptly.
   b. oversee the general operation of the office.
   c. hire and fire other office staff.
   d. plan the office Christmas party.

After you eliminate *a* and *d* because they are clearly not primary responsibilities, you can look at both of the others in a true/false context.

The primary responsibility of the office manager is to oversee the general operation of the office. True or false?

The primary responsibility of the office manager is to hire and fire other staff. True or false?

Between these two it seems clear that the truer of the statements is that the manager oversees general operations. While he or she may participate in hiring decisions, it is unlikely that it is his or her primary responsibility. Notice that the key word in the stem is *primary*.

This strategy is particularly helpful when you are given options such as all of the above, none of the above, or only 2 and 4 above.

MANAGING YOUR TIME ON THE MULTIPLE-CHOICE TEST

It's important to manage your time so that you don't get stuck on any one question. The following section will help you pace yourself so that you increase your chances for getting all the points you can get in the time you are allowed.

READ OR LISTEN TO DIRECTIONS CAREFULLY

If you are allowed, always underline or circle key words in the instructions that cue you to what the question requires. Follow the directions to the letter.

PREVIEW THE TEST

There should be no surprises when you get to any section of the test. It's always helpful to know what you will encounter on the test.

There are two reasons that you should preview a test very carefully before you start working:

- You want to find out where rough spots are on the test, so that you can prepare to spend more time on those sections.
- You want to be familiar with the content of the whole test so that you have a good overall picture of what topics are stressed and know the formats for all of the sections of the test. Then as you go back and work through the test, you're revisiting familiar ground.

DON'T LINGER TOO LONG ON ANY ONE QUESTION

Answer the questions in a section or on the whole test that you know the answers to for certain right away. If you are unsure about a question, put a dot in the margin next to that question so that you can find it easily when you want to come back to it later. Don't linger too long over questions you can't answer right away. You may find that other questions on the test will steer you to the best choices for questions that at first seem difficult to you.

HOW TO AVOID PANIC

There are times when you may feel absolutely panicked in the middle of a test. If you are feeling shaky because you see too many unfamiliar questions on the test, are running out of time, or have just run out of energy for a while, here are some techniques for keeping yourself from coming unglued:

- Stop writing for a minute or two and relax.
- Sit back in your chair. Let your arms and head drop down and breathe slowly and deeply for a few seconds.
- Try to empty your mind of all its worries and visualize the end of the test.
- Stretch your arms, hands, neck, and shoulders.
- Return to the test with a "get tough" attitude.

WHEN YOU HAVE TIME LEFT OVER

If you've followed the suggestions in these chapters and conscientiously maintained control over the timing, you may find that you have time left over after you have finished the test. Do not throw down your pen and sigh with relief that the test is over—at least not yet. Remember, this is not a race. You don't win by being first over the finish line. Resist the temptation to leave right away. Here are some suggestions for making the best possible use of any time left over:

- **Don't leave anything out.** Double-check that you didn't miss any questions and you have answers for any questions you may have skipped the first time through the test. Use the tips you learned about guessing on multiple-choice tests to help you make an educated guess on any questions about which you are still uncertain.
- **Double-check your answers.** Make sure each answer you've chosen is entered on the correct spot on the answer sheet and is legibly written. If you change an answer, make sure you change it completely.

Now you know how to deal with multiple-choice tests. The strategies you've learned should help you to prepare for, take, and excel on the ASVAB. You should be able to manage your test day and get into the military with confidence. The rest of the sections in this book will help you prepare specific skills for the Arithmetic Reasoning, Mathematics Knowledge, Paragraph Comprehension, and Word Knowledge portions of the ASVAB.

MATH FOR THE ARITHMETIC REASONING AND MATHEMATICS KNOWLEDGE SUBTESTS

The Arithmetic Reasoning and Mathematics Knowledge subtests of the ASVAB cover math skills. Arithmetic Reasoning is mostly made up of math word problems. Mathematics Knowledge tests knowledge of math concepts, principles, and procedures. You don't have to do a lot of calculation in the Mathematics Knowledge subtest; you need to know basic terminology (like sum and perimeter), formulas (such as the area of a square), and computation rules. Both subtests cover the subjects you might have studied in school. This section of the book reviews concepts you'll need for both Arithmetic Reasoning and Mathematics Knowledge.

MATH STRATEGIES

- Don't work in your head! Use your test book or scratch paper to take notes, draw pictures, and calculate. Although you might think that you can solve math questions more quickly in your head, that's a good way to make mistakes. Write out each step.

- Read a math question in chunks rather than straight through from beginning to end. As you read each chunk, stop to think about what it means and make notes or draw a picture to represent that chunk.

- When you get to the actual question of the problem, underline it. This will keep you more focused as you solve the problem.
- Glance at the answer choices for clues. If they're fractions, you probably should do your work in fractions; if they're decimals, you should probably work in decimals, and so on.
- Make a plan of attack to help you solve the problem.
- If a question stumps you, try working backward—it can be particularly useful for solving word problems.
- When you get your answer, reread the question you underlined to make sure you've answered it. This will help you avoid the careless mistake of answering the wrong question.
- Check your work after you get an answer. Test-takers get a false sense of security when they get an answer that matches one of the multiple-choice answers. Here are some good ways to check your work if you have time:
  - Ask yourself if your answer is reasonable; does it makes sense?
  - Plug your answer back into the problem to make sure the problem holds together.
  - Do the question a second time, but use a different method.
- Skip hard questions and come back to them later. Mark them in your test book so you can find them quickly.

GLOSSARY OF MATH TERMS TO KNOW FOR THE ASVAB

Circumference	The circumference is the continuous curved line of a circle. Every point on the curved line is the same distance from the center.
Denominator	The bottom number in a fraction. Example: 2 is the denominator in $\frac{1}{2}$.
Diameter	The diameter is the line through the center of a circle.
Difference	The difference of two numbers is the answer to a subtraction problem.
Divisible by	A number is divisible by another number if the result of the division is a whole number and the remainder is zero. For example: $\frac{10}{5} = 2$ therefore, 10 is divisible by 5.
Dividend	The quantity to be divided in a division problem.
Divisor	The number of equal parts the dividend is to be divided into in a division problem.
Even Number	A number that is divisible by 2.
Factor	The numbers multiplied in a multiplication problem.
Integer	Every whole number on the number line, both positive and negative.
Multiple of	A number that is the product of a given number and a whole number. For example: Multiples of 3 are 3, 6, 9, 12, 15, and so on.
Negative Number	A number that is less than zero, like -1, -18.6, or $-\frac{1}{2}$
Numerator	The top part of a fraction. For example: 1 is the numerator of $\frac{1}{2}$.
Odd Number	A number that isn't divisible by 2.
Perimeter	The distance around a polygon, such as a triangle or a rectangle. The perimeter is the sum of the lengths of all sides of a polygon.
Polygon	Any flat figure with three or more connected sides. Triangles, squares, and rectangles are the most common polygons, but polygons can have five, six, seven, and more sides.
Positive Number	A number that is greater than zero, like 2, $\frac{1}{4}$, 6.5.
Prime Number	An integer that is divisible only by 1 and itself, like 2, 3, 5, 7, 11, and so on.
Product	The result of multiplying one number by another.
Radius	The line segment from the center of the circle to any point on the circumference of the circle. The radius is one half of the diameter.
Quotient	The answer in a division problem. For example: $\frac{15}{3} = 5$.
Remainder	An amount that is left over when you find a quotient.
Sum	The answer to an addition problem. For example: $5 + 2 = 7$.

L·E·S·S·O·N 4
BASIC ARITHMETIC FUNCTIONS

ADDING WHOLE NUMBERS

When we add numbers, we are putting together two or more groups to find the total. The total is often called the sum. For example, suppose you have 5 cans of soup in your kitchen cupboard, and you buy 4 more. Now you have a total of 9 cans of soup. The number 9 is the sum (total), of the two groups.

Now, suppose you want to add two or more larger groups. To add larger numbers correctly, follow these simple rules:

1. Line up the numbers in a straight column. Arrange the numbers according to place value.
2. Add each column. Start the addition at the right with the ones column.
3. Make sure your answers are in the correct columns.

Example: At the store where you buy your soup, there are 132 cans on the shelves. The stocker adds 56 more cans. You want to know how many cans there are in all. The problem, written out, would look like this: 132 + 56. To find the answer, follow the three steps:

1. Line up the numbers in a straight column.

132 = 1 hundred 3 tens 2 ones

+56 =   5 tens 6 ones

2. Add each column. Start the addition at the right with the ones column:

1 hundred 3 tens 2 ones

+   5 tens 6 ones

    1   8   8

3. Make sure your answers are in the correct columns:

132 = 1 hundred 3 tens 2 ones

+56 =   5 tens 6 ones

188 = 1 hundred 8 tens 8 ones

Copy the numbers into columns and add.

_____ **1.** 567 + 12

_____ **2.** 3,004 + 1,790

_____ **3.** 24 + 831

_____ **4.** 22 + 513 + 104

_____ **5.** 1,526 + 40

_____ **6.** 10,412 + 30 + 1,547

CARRYING

When you add a column of numbers, the sum may be 10 or more. For example, if your ones column adds up to 14, you have a total of 1 ten and 4 ones. Now you must carry the 1 to the tens column.

To carry, follow these simple rules:

1. Line up the numbers to be added in a straight column.
2. Add the numbers in the ones place.
3. If the sum is 10 or more, write the number in the tens place at the top of the next column.
4. Add the tens column, starting with the number you carried.

5. Add the other columns in the same way.

Example: 238 + 76

1. Line up the numbers to be added in a straight column:

238

+76

2. Add the numbers in the ones place:

6

+8

14

3. If the sum is 10 or more, carry the number in the tens place to the top of the next column:

1

238

+76

4

4. Add the tens column, starting with the number you carried:

1

3

+7

11

5. Add the other columns in the same way:

1 1

238

+76

314

Copy the numbers into columns and add.

_____ **7.** 499 + 78

_____ **8.** 16 + 9 + 27

_____ **9.** 1,465 + 2,808

_____ **10.** 367 + 20,553

_____ **11.** 351 + 42 + 86 + 5

_____ **12.** 19 + 1,600 + 782 + 62

SUBTRACTING

When you subtract two numbers, you are finding the difference between them.

Here are some questions answered by subtraction:

- When we take 4 away from 9, how many are left?
- What is the difference between 4 and 9?
- What is 9 minus 4?
- How much more is 9 than 4?
- To get 9, how much must be added to 4?

To subtract, follow these simple rules:

1. Line up the numbers in a column. Arrange the numbers according to place value.
2. Start the subtraction at the right with the ones column.
3. Make sure your answers are in the correct columns.

Example: 98 − 75

1. Line up the numbers in a column. Arrange the numbers according to place value:

   98 =   9 tens and 8 ones
   −75 = −7 tens and 5 ones

2. Start the subtraction at the right with the ones column:

   9 tens and 8 ones
   −7 tens and 5 ones
   _____
        2   3

3. Make sure your answers are in the correct columns:

   98 =   9 tens and 8 ones
   −75 = −7 tens and 5 ones
   _____
   23   2 tens and 3 ones

Copy the numbers into columns and subtract.

_____**13.** 48 − 17   _____**16.** 992 − 61

_____**14.** 79 − 39   _____**17.** 3,667 − 2,005

_____**15.** 156 − 44   _____**18.** 235 − 112

BORROWING

Sometimes the top number in a column is larger than the bottom number. Then you must borrow from the next column. Borrowing is also known as regrouping.

To borrow, follow these simple rules:

1. Line up the columns by place value, as usual.
2. Start with the right column, the ones place. If you cannot subtract the bottom number from the top number, borrow from the tens place. Write the new numbers at the top of each column.
3. Continue subtracting from right to left.
4. Optional: Check the result by adding.

Example: 52 − 36

1. Line up the columns by place value, as usual:

   52 =   5 tens and 2 ones
   −36 = − 3 tens and 6 ones

2. Start with the right column, the ones place. If you cannot subtract the bottom number from the top number, borrow from the tens place. (Since you cannot subtract 6 from 2, you must

borrow from the 5 in the tens place.) Write the new numbers at the top of each column:

4 12 =   4 tens and   12 ones
~~52 =   5 tens and 2 ones~~
−36 = −3 tens and 6 ones

Notice that you are taking 1 ten (10 ones) and adding it to the ones place. Now you have 12 ones: $2 + 10 = 12$. You have also taken one ten away from the tens place: $5 − 1 = 4$.

3. Continue subtracting from right to left:

4 12
~~52~~
−36
16

4. Optional: Check the result by adding:
$16 + 36 = 52$.

Practice

_____**19.** 37 − 28   _____**22.** 465 − 277
_____**20.** 61 − 14   _____**23.** 1,381 − 497
_____**21.** 193 − 88   _____**24.** 22,623 − 13,884

MULTIPLYING WHOLE NUMBERS

Multiplication is the short method of adding a number to itself several times. (The sign for multiplication is x) For example, 4 x 2, read "4 times 2" means "2 + 2 + 2 + 2." If you add 4 twos together, you will get a total of 8. So $4 \times 2 = 8$. In multiplication, the two numbers multiplied are called factors. The result of multiplying one number by another is called the product. This means that 8 is the product of 4 times 2.

We use multiplication to put together equal groups. Suppose you had 3 packs of gum. Each pack has 5 sticks. You have 3 groups of 5. You want to find out how many sticks of gum you have altogether. You could add 5 + 5 + 5. But a shorter way is multiply 3 times 5.

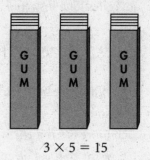

$3 \times 5 = 15$

Sometimes it is helpful to view equal groups in rows or columns. If you add all the blocks in the figure below, you will get a total of 24. A shorter way is to multiply. There are 4 blocks in the rows across. There are 6 blocks in the up-and-down rows.

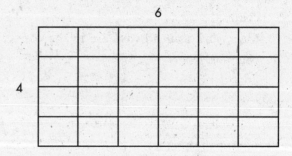

$4 \times 6 = 24$

MULTIPLICATION TABLE

It is important that you commit to memory all the multiplication facts up to 12. Below is a multiplication table to help you. The second row across will give you the result of all the numbers multiplied by 1 ($1 \times 1 = 1$; $1 \times 2 = 2$; $1 \times 3 = 3$; and so forth). The next row will give you the result of all the numbers multiplied by 2 ($2 \times 1 = 2$; $2 \times 2 = 4$). Memorize the multiplication table before you read the next math chapters.

	1	2	3	4	5	6	7	8	9	10	11	12
1	1	2	3	4	5	6	7	8	9	10	11	12
2	2	4	6	8	10	12	14	16	18	20	22	24
3	3	6	9	12	15	18	21	24	27	30	33	36
4	4	8	12	16	20	24	28	32	36	40	44	48
5	5	10	15	20	25	30	35	40	45	50	55	60
6	6	12	18	24	30	36	42	48	54	60	66	72
7	7	14	21	28	35	42	49	56	63	70	77	84
8	8	16	24	32	40	48	56	64	72	80	88	96
9	9	18	27	36	45	54	63	72	81	90	99	108
10	10	20	30	40	50	60	70	80	90	100	110	120
11	11	22	33	44	55	66	77	88	99	110	121	132
12	12	24	36	48	60	72	84	96	108	120	132	144

Here are a few more tips to help you learn multiplication.

- You may have already noticed that the order of the numbers (factors) doesn't change the result: $7 \times 2 = 14$ and $2 \times 7 = 14$. In other words, 7 groups of 2 equals 2 groups of 7.
- In multiplication, when one of the factors is zero, the product is zero: $7 \times 0 = 0$ and $0 \times 7 = 0$. This is true no matter how large the number is: $1 \times 0 = 0$ and $1,000,000 \times 0 = 0$.

MULTIPLYING BY ONE-DIGIT NUMBERS

To multiply whole numbers:

1. Line up the numbers by place value.
2. Begin multiplying in the ones place. If necessary, carry to the next column.
3. Continue multiplying from right to left. Add any numbers that were "carried."

Example: 6 × 27

1. Line up the numbers by place value:

   27

   × 6

2. Begin multiplying in the ones place. If necessary carry to the next column. (6 × 7 = 42. Carry 4 tens to the tens place.)

   4
   27
   × 6
   2

3. Continue multiplying from right to left. Add any numbers that were carried. (6 × 2 = 12 and 12 + 4 = 16):

   4
   27
   × 6
   162

Multiply

_____**25.** 63 × 2   _____**28.** 109 × 8

_____**26.** 79 × 7   _____**29.** 530 × 6

_____**27.** 48 × 3   _____**30.** 800 × 9

MULTIPLYING BY NUMBERS WITH TWO OR MORE DIGITS

The following will help you learn to multiply with two (or more) digit numbers. There are three steps.

1. Multiply as usual by the number in the ones place.
2. Multiply by the number in the tens place. (For larger numbers continue to line up the numbers according to place value.) Write this product (result) in the tens place under the first product.
3. Add the columns.

Example: 34 x 26

1. Multiply as usual by the number in the ones place:(6 × 34 = 204)

   2
   34
   × 26
   204

2. Multiply by the number in the tens place. Write this product (result) in the tens place under the first product. If you want, you can put a zero in the ones place as a place holder. (2 × 34 = 68):

   34
   × 26
   204
   680

Note that the 8 is aligned with the 2 in the multiplier and that the zero serves as a place holder so that you align the numbers correctly. (To multiply with three (or more) digit numbers, multiply the third product in the hundreds place.)

3. Add the columns:

   34
   × 26
   204
   + 680
   884

Multiply

_____**31.** 77 × 11   _____**34.** 456 × 53

_____**32.** 98 × 32   _____**35.** 612 × 22

_____**33.** 85 × 45   _____**36.** 128 × 141

DIVIDING WHOLE NUMBERS

Division means dividing an amount into equal groups. Suppose you have 12 cookies. You want to divide them equally among 3 people. You want 3 groups out of a total of 12. To do this, you need to use division.

$$12 \div 3 = 4$$

When you divide 12 equally into 3 groups, you have 4 in each group. The sign $\div$ means "divided by."

DIVISION IS THE OPPOSITE OF MULTIPLICATION

You learned earlier that subtraction is the opposite of addition. Division is the opposite of multiplication:

$$12 \div 3 = 4 \text{ and } 4 \times 3 = 12.$$

You need practice to learn basic division facts. Memorize them as you did multiplication. You can use the multiplication table as a guide. Read it in reverse.

THE LANGUAGE OF DIVISION

The quantity to be divided is called the dividend. The number of equal parts is called the divisor. The result is called the quotient.

40 (dividend) $\div$ 5 (divisor) = 8 (quotient)

Another way to write out this problem would be:

$$5 \overline{)40} \quad \overset{8}{}$$

One more way to write this problem would be: $\frac{40}{5} = 8$

MORE TO REMEMBER ABOUT DIVISION

When you divide any number by itself, the result is 1: $8 \div 8 = 1$

When you divide any number by 1, the result is the number itself: $8 \div 1 = 8$

When zero is divided by another number, the result is zero: $0 \div 8 = 0$

DIVIDING BY ONE-DIGIT NUMBERS

There are several steps to division. In these steps you will use addition, subtraction, and multiplication.

Here are the steps to division:

1. Write the problem correctly.
2. Estimate and divide.
3. Write your answer on top.
4. Multiply and write your answer below.
5. Subtract.
6. Bring down.
7. Repeat the steps if necessary.

Example: $216 \div 9$

1. Write the problem correctly:

$$9 \overline{)216}$$

2. Estimate and divide: You cannot divide 9 into 2. So you must divide 9 into 21. Think about how many times 9 will go into 21. $9 \times 3 = 27$ is too large, so try 2.

3. Write your answer on top:

$$\begin{array}{r} 2 \\ 9\overline{)216} \end{array}$$

Notice that your answer is written above the tens place. (If you are able to divide evenly into the hundreds place, the answer is written above the hundreds place.)

4. Multiply ($9 \times 2 = 18$) and write your answer below:

$$\begin{array}{r} 2 \\ 9\overline{)216} \\ 18 \end{array}$$

5. Subtract ($21 - 18 = 3$):

$$\begin{array}{r} 2 \\ 9\overline{)216} \\ -18 \\ \hline 3 \end{array}$$

6. Bring down (6):

$$\begin{array}{r} 2 \\ 9\overline{)216} \\ -18 \\ \hline 36 \end{array}$$

7. Repeat the steps if necessary ($36 \div 9 = 4$):

$$\begin{array}{r} 24 \\ 9\overline{)216} \\ -18 \\ \hline 36 \\ -36 \\ \hline 0 \end{array}$$

REMAINDERS

Sometimes the quotient (answer) will not be exact. You will have a number left over. This number is called a remainder. This means that you have a certain number of equal groups with one or more left over. Let's say you have 13 cookies instead of 12. You want to divide them into 3 groups. You will still have 3 groups of 4. But now you will have one cookie remaining. You can show that there is a remainder by writing an R and the number left over beside the answer. $13 \div 3 = 4R1$

CHECKING YOUR WORK

To check your work in division:

1. Multiply your answer (the quotient) by the divisor.
2. Add any remainder. Is your answer the dividend (the number you divided into)? Then your work is correct.

Divide.

_____ **37.** $65 \div 5$ _____ **40.** $188 \div 3$

_____ **38.** $256 \div 4$ _____ **41.** $5511 \div 4$

_____ **39.** $37 \div 6$ _____ **42.** $2929 \div 9$

DIVIDING BY TWO- OR THREE-DIGIT NUMBERS

The steps for dividing by two- or three-digit numbers are the same. However, you are dividing by a larger number in the first step.

Divide.

_____ **43.** $325 \div 25$ _____ **46.** $4,207 \div 18$

_____ **44.** $381 \div 127$ _____ **47.** $40,000 \div 20$

_____ **45.** $1,941 \div 96$ _____ **48.** $11,000 \div 550$

ANSWERS

1. 579
2. 855
3. 1,566
4. 4,794
5. 639
6. 11,989
7. 577
8. 52
9. 4,273
10. 20,920
11. 484
12. 2,463
13. 31
14. 40
15. 112
16. 931
17. 1662
18. 123
19. 9
20. 47
21. 105
22. 188
23. 884
24. 8739
25. 126
26. 553
27. 144
28. 872
29. 3,180
30. 7,200
31. 847
32. 3,136
33. 3,825
34. 24,168
35. 13,464
36. 18,048
37. 13
38. 64
39. 6 R1
40. 62 R2
41. 1377 R3
42. 325 R4
43. 13
44. 3
45. 20 R21
46. 233 R13
47. 2,000
48. 20

FRACTIONS, DECIMALS, PERCENTS, AND AVERAGES

FRACTIONS

A fraction is a part of a whole. Let's say that a pizza was cut into 8 equal slices and you ate 3 of them. The fraction $\frac{3}{8}$ tells you what part of the pizza you ate. The pizza below shows this: 3 of the 8 pieces (the ones you ate) are shaded.

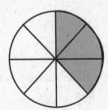

There are two numbers in this simple fraction. They are called the *numerator* and the *denominator*. The *numerator* is the top number of the fraction. The *denominator* is the bottom number. In the fraction $\frac{3}{8}$, the numerator is 3 and the denominator is 8.

$$\frac{3}{8} = \frac{\text{numerator}}{\text{denominator}} = \frac{\text{number of parts being considered}}{\text{equal parts in the whole}}$$

Here are some other examples of fractions:

- An hour is a fraction of a day. There are 24 equal parts in a day. An hour is one of those parts. So, an hour is $\frac{1}{24}$ of an day.
- Weights are expressed in fractions. There are 16 ounces in a pound. Five ounces would be $\frac{5}{16}$ of a pound.

- Money is expressed in fractions. There are 10 dimes in one dollar. So, 70 cents, or 7 dimes, is $\frac{7}{10}$ of a dollar.

THREE KINDS OF FRACTIONS

- Proper fraction: The top number is less than the bottom number:
$\frac{1}{2}; \frac{2}{3}; \frac{4}{9}; \frac{8}{13}$
The value of a proper fraction is less than 1.

- Improper fraction: The top number is greater than or equal to the bottom number:
$\frac{3}{2}; \frac{5}{3}; \frac{14}{9}; \frac{12}{12}$
The value of an improper fraction is 1 or more.

  - When the top number and the bottom number are the same, the fraction is equal to 1. For example, $\frac{2}{2}; \frac{5}{5}; \frac{144}{144}$.

  - When the top number is greater than the bottom number, the fraction is equal to more than 1. For example, $\frac{3}{2}; \frac{7}{4}; \frac{10}{9}$.

  - If the bottom number of the fraction is 1, that improper fraction is the same as a whole number. For example, $\frac{2}{1} = 2; \frac{10}{1} = 10; \frac{144}{1} = 144$.

- Mixed number: A fraction written to the right of a whole number:
$3\frac{1}{2}; 4\frac{2}{3}; 12\frac{3}{4}; 24\frac{3}{4}$
The value of a mixed number is more than 1: it is the sum of the whole number plus the fraction.

CHANGING IMPROPER FRACTIONS INTO MIXED OR WHOLE NUMBERS

It's easier to add and subtract fractions that are mixed numbers rather than improper fractions. To change an improper fraction, say $\frac{13}{2}$, into a mixed number, follow these steps:

1. Divide the denominator (2) into the numerator (13) to get the whole number portion (6) of the mixed number:

$$2\overline{)13} \quad \begin{array}{r} 6 \text{ R1} \\ -12 \\ \hline 1 \end{array}$$

2. Write the remainder of the division (1) over the old denominator (2): $6\frac{1}{2}$

3. Check: Change the mixed number back into an improper fraction (see steps below).

CHANGING MIXED NUMBERS INTO IMPROPER FRACTIONS

It's easier to multiply and divide fractions when you're working with improper fractions rather than mixed numbers. To change a mixed number, say $2\frac{3}{4}$, into an improper fraction, follow these steps:

1. Multiply the whole number (2) by the bottom number (4): $2 \times 4 = 8$

2. Add the result (8) to the numerator (3):
$8 + 3 = 11$

3. Put the total (11) over the denominator (4):
$\frac{11}{4}$

4. Check: Reverse the process by changing the improper fraction into a mixed number. If you get back the number you started with, your answer is right.

REDUCING FRACTIONS

Reducing a fraction means writing it in lowest terms, that is, with smaller numbers. For instance, 50¢ is $\frac{50}{100}$ of a dollar, or $\frac{1}{2}$ of a dollar. In fact, if you have 50¢ in your pocket, you say that you have half a dollar. Reducing a fraction does not change its value.

Follow these steps to reduce a fraction:

1. Find a whole number that divides evenly into both numbers that make up the fraction.
2. Divide that number into the top of the fraction, and replace the top of the fraction with the quotient (the answer you got when you divided).
3. Do the same thing to the bottom number.
4. Repeat the first 3 steps until you can't find a number that divides evenly into both numbers of the fraction.

For example, let's reduce $\frac{8}{24}$.

- We could do it in 2 steps: $\frac{8 \div 4}{24 \div 4} = \frac{2}{6}$; then $\frac{2 \div 2}{6 \div 2} = \frac{1}{3}$.
- Or, we could do it in a single step: $\frac{8 \div 8}{24 \div 8}$.

Shortcut: When both the numerator and denominator end in zeroes, cross out the same number of zeroes in both numbers to begin the reducing process. For example, $\frac{300}{4000}$ reduces to $\frac{3}{40}$ when you cross out 2 zeroes in both numbers.

Whenever you do arithmetic with fractions, reduce your answer. On a multiple-choice test, don't panic if your answer isn't listed. Try to reduce it further and then compare it to the choices.

Reduce these fractions to lowest terms:

1. $\frac{3}{12}$

2. $\frac{14}{35}$

3. $\frac{27}{72}$

RAISING FRACTIONS TO HIGHER TERMS

Before you can add and subtract fractions, you have to know how to raise a fraction to higher terms. This is actually the opposite of reducing a fraction.

$\frac{1}{2} = \frac{2}{4}$, but $\frac{1}{2}$ is also equal to $\frac{4}{8}$ or $\frac{5}{10}$, or $\frac{25}{50}$.

Follow these steps to raise $\frac{2}{3}$ to 24ths:

1. Divide the original denominator (3) into the number you want to make the new denominator (24): $24 \div 3 = 8$
2. Multiply your answer (8) by the numerator (2): $2 \times 8 = 16$
3. Put your answer (16) over the new denominator (24): $\frac{16}{24}$
4. Check: Reduce the new fraction to see if you get back the original one: $\frac{(16 \div 8)}{(24 \div 8)} = \frac{2}{3}$

Raise these fractions to higher terms:

4. $\frac{5}{12} = \frac{}{24}$

5. $\frac{2}{9} = \frac{}{27}$

6. $\frac{2}{5} = \frac{}{500}$

ADDING FRACTIONS

If the fractions have the same denominator, just add the numerators together and write the total over the denominator.

Examples: $\frac{2}{9} + \frac{4}{9} = \frac{2+4}{9} = \frac{6}{9}$

Reduce the sum: $\frac{2}{3}$

$\frac{5}{8} + \frac{7}{8} = \frac{12}{8}$

Change the sum to a mixed number: $1\frac{4}{8}$

Then reduce: $1\frac{1}{2}$

There are a few extra steps to add mixed numbers with the same denominator, say $2\frac{3}{5} + 1\frac{4}{5}$:

1. Add the fractions: $\frac{3}{5} + \frac{4}{5} = \frac{7}{5}$

2. Change the improper fraction into a mixed number: $\frac{7}{5} = 1\frac{2}{5}$

3. Add the whole numbers: $2 + 1 = 3$

4. Add the results of steps 2 and 3:
$1\frac{2}{5} + 3 = 4\frac{2}{5}$

FINDING THE LEAST COMMON DENOMINATOR

In order to add fractions with different denominators, you'll need to find the smallest number that both fractions can use as a denominator, the *least common denominator*.

Here are a few tips for finding the LCD, the smallest number that all the bottom numbers evenly divide into:

- See if all the bottom numbers divide evenly into the biggest bottom number.

- Think of numbers, and check the multiplication table on page 43 to find a number that all the other bottom numbers evenly divide into.

- When all else fails, multiply all the bottom numbers together.

Example: $\frac{2}{3} + \frac{4}{5}$

1. Find the LCD. Multiply the bottom numbers:
$3 \times 5 = 15$

2. Raise each fraction to 15ths:
$\frac{2}{3}\left(\frac{5}{5}\right) = \frac{10}{15}$
$\frac{4}{5}\left(\frac{3}{3}\right) = \frac{12}{15}$

3. Add as usual: $\frac{10}{15} + \frac{12}{15} = \frac{22}{15}$

Add these fractions:

7. $\frac{3}{4} + \frac{1}{6}$
8. $\frac{7}{8} + \frac{2}{3} + \frac{3}{4}$
9. $4\frac{1}{3} + 2\frac{3}{4} + \frac{1}{6}$

SUBTRACTING FRACTIONS

If the fractions have the same bottom numbers, just subtract the top numbers and write the difference over the bottom number.

Example: $\frac{4}{9} - \frac{3}{9} = \frac{4-3}{9} = \frac{1}{9}$

If the fractions you want to subtract don't have the same bottom number, you'll have to raise some or all of the fractions to higher terms so that they all have the same bottom number, or LCD. If you forgot how to find the LCD, just read the section on adding fractions with different bottom numbers.

Example: $\frac{5}{6} - \frac{3}{4}$

1. Raise each fraction to 12ths because 12 is the LCD, the smallest number that 6 and 4 both divide into evenly: $\frac{5}{6}\left(\frac{2}{2}\right) = \frac{10}{12}$
   $$\frac{3}{4}\left(\frac{3}{3}\right) = -\frac{9}{12}$$
2. Subtract as usual: $\frac{10}{12} - \frac{9}{12} = \frac{1}{12}$

Subtracting mixed numbers with the same bottom number is similar to adding mixed numbers.

Example: $4\frac{3}{5} - 1\frac{2}{5}$

1. Subtract the fractions: $\frac{3}{5} - \frac{2}{5} = \frac{1}{5}$
2. Subtract the whole numbers: $4 - 1 = 3$
3. Add the results of steps 1 and 2: $\frac{1}{5} + 3 = 3\frac{1}{5}$

Sometimes there is an extra "borrowing" step when you subtract mixed numbers with the same bottom numbers, say $7\frac{3}{5} - 2\frac{4}{5}$:

1. You can't subtract the fractions the way they are because $\frac{4}{5}$ is bigger than $\frac{3}{5}$. So you borrow 1 from the 7, making it 6. and change that 1 to $\frac{5}{5}$ because 5 is the bottom number: $7\frac{3}{5} = 6\frac{5}{5} + \frac{3}{5}$
2. Add the numbers from step 1: $6\frac{5}{5} + \frac{3}{5} = 6\frac{8}{5}$
3. Now you have a different version of the original problem: $6\frac{8}{5} - 2\frac{4}{5}$
4. Subtract the fractional parts of the two mixed numbers: $\frac{8}{5} - \frac{4}{5} = \frac{4}{5}$
5. Subtract the whole number parts of the two mixed numbers: $6 - 2 = 4$
6. Add the results of the last 2 steps together: $4 + \frac{4}{5} = 4\frac{4}{5}$

Try these subtraction problems:

10. $\frac{4}{5} - \frac{2}{3}$

11. $\frac{7}{8} - \frac{1}{4} - \frac{1}{2}$

12. $4\frac{1}{3} - 2\frac{3}{4}$

MULTIPLYING FRACTIONS

Multiplying fractions is actually easier than adding them. All you do is multiply the top numbers and then multiply the bottom numbers.

Examples: $\frac{2}{3} \times \frac{5}{7} = \frac{2 \times 5}{3 \times 7} = \frac{10}{21}$

$$\frac{1}{2} \times \frac{3}{5} \times \frac{7}{4} = \frac{1 \times 3 \times 7}{2 \times 5 \times 4} = \frac{21}{40}$$

Sometimes you can cancel before multiplying. Canceling will save you time because you multiply with smaller numbers. It's very similar to reducing: Look for a number that will divide evenly into the numerator of one fraction and the denominator of the other. Do the division before you multiply. You will get the same answer with the smaller numbers as you did with the larger numbers. But the smaller numbers will save you time.

Example: $\frac{5}{6} \times \frac{9}{20}$

1. Cancel the 6 and the 9 by dividing 3 into both of them: $6 \div 3 = 2$ and $9 \div 3 = 3$. Cross out the 6 and the 9 and replace them with the smaller numbers.

$$\frac{5}{\underset{2}{\cancel{6}}} \times \frac{\overset{3}{\cancel{9}}}{20}$$

2. Cancel the 5 and the 20 by dividing 5 into both of them: $5 \div 5 = 1$ and $20 \div 5 = 4$. Cross out the 5 and the 20.

$$\frac{\cancel{5}^{\,1}}{2} \times \frac{3}{\cancel{20}_{\,4}}$$

3. Multiply across the new top numbers and the new bottom numbers:

$$\frac{1 \times 3}{2 \times 4} = \frac{3}{8}$$

Try these multiplication problems:

13. $\frac{1}{5} \times \frac{2}{3}$

14. $\frac{2}{3} \times \frac{4}{7} \times \frac{3}{5}$

15. $\frac{3}{4} \times \frac{8}{9}$

To multiply with whole mixed numbers, it's easier to change them to improper fractions before multiplying.

Try these multiplication problems with mixed numbers and whole numbers:

16. $4\frac{1}{3} \times \frac{2}{5}$

17. $2\frac{1}{2} \times 6$

18. $3\frac{3}{4} \times 4\frac{2}{5}$

DIVIDING FRACTIONS

To divide one fraction by a second fraction, invert the second fraction (that is, flip the top and bottom numbers) and then multiply. That's all there is to it!

Example: $\frac{1}{2} \div \frac{3}{5}$

1. Invert the second fraction ($\frac{3}{5}$): $\frac{5}{3}$

2. Change the division sign ($\div$) to a multiplication sign ($\times$)

3. Multiply the first fraction by the new second fraction: $\frac{1}{2} \times \frac{5}{3} = \frac{1 \times 5}{2 \times 3} = \frac{5}{6}$

When the division problem has a mixed or a whole number, convert it to an improper fraction and then divide as usual.

Divide these fractions:

19. $\frac{1}{3} \div \frac{2}{3}$

20. $\frac{23}{4} \div \frac{1}{2}$

21. $\frac{3}{5} \div 3$

DECIMALS

A decimal is a special kind of fraction. You use decimals every day when you deal with money—$10.35 is a decimal that represents 10 dollars and 35 cents. The decimal point separates the dollars from the cents. Because there are 100 cents in one dollar, 1¢ is $\frac{1}{100}$ of a dollar, or $.01.

$.1 = 1$ tenth $= \frac{1}{10}$
$.02 = 2$ hundredths $= \frac{2}{100}$
$.003 = 3$ thousandths $= \frac{3}{1000}$
$.0004 = 4$ ten-thousandths $= \frac{4}{10,000}$

When you add zeroes after the rightmost decimal place, you don't change the value of the decimal. For example, 6.17 is the same as all of these:

6.170
6.1700
6.17000000000000000

If there are digits on both sides of the decimal point (like 10.35), the number is called a mixed decimal. If there are digits only to the right of the decimal point (like .53), the number is called a decimal.

CHANGING FRACTIONS TO DECIMALS

To change a fraction to a decimal, divide the bottom number into the top number after you put a decimal point and a few zeroes on the right of the top number. When you divide, bring the decimal point up into your answer.

Example: Change $\frac{3}{4}$ to a decimal.

1. Set up a long division problem to divide the top number into the bottom number, but don't divide yet (3):

$$4\overline{)3}$$

2. Add a decimal point and a few zeroes to the right of the divisor (the number you are dividing into: 3.00
   Bring the decimal point up into the answer and divide:

$$
\begin{array}{r}
.75 \\
4\overline{)3.00} \\
-28 \\
\hline
20 \\
-20 \\
\hline
0
\end{array}
$$

3. The quotient (result of the division) is the answer: .75

Some fractions may require you to add many decimal zeroes in order for the division to come out evenly.

When you convert a fraction like $\frac{2}{3}$ to a decimal, you can keep adding decimal zeroes to the top number

forever because the division will never come out evenly! As you divide 3 into 2, you'll keep getting 6s: $2 \div 3 =$ .6666666666 etc. This is called a repeating decimal and it can be written as .666 or as .66$\frac{2}{3}$. You can approximate it as .67, .667, .6667, and so on.

CHANGING DECIMALS TO FRACTIONS

To change a decimal to a fraction, write the digits of the decimal as the top number of a fraction and write the decimal's name as the bottom number of the fraction. Then reduce the fraction, if possible.

Example: .018

1. Write 18 as the top of the fraction: $\frac{18}{}$
2. Three places to the right of the decimal means thousandths, so write 1,000 as the bottom number: $\frac{18}{1000}$
3. Reduce by dividing 2 into the top and bottom numbers: $\frac{18 \div 2}{1000 \div 2} = \frac{9}{500}$

Change these decimals or mixed decimals to fractions:

22. .005

23. 3.48

24. 123.456

ADDING AND SUBTRACTING DECIMALS

To add or subtract decimals, line them up so their decimal points are even. You may want to tack on zeroes at the end of shorter decimals so you can keep all your digits lined up evenly. Remember, if a number doesn't have a decimal point, you can add one at the right end of the number.

Example: $1.23 + 57 + .038$

Line up the numbers, then add:

```
  1.230
 57.000
+  .038
 58.268
```

Example: $1.23 - .038$

Line up the numbers, then subtract:

```
 1.230
 -.038
 1.192
```

Try these addition and subtraction problems:

25. $.905 + .02 + 3.075$
26. $.005 + 8 + .3$
27. $3.48 - 2.573$

MULTIPLYING DECIMALS

To multiply decimals, ignore the decimal points and just multiply the numbers. Then count the total number of decimal digits (the digits to the right of the decimal point) in all of the numbers you're multiplying. Count off that number of digits in your answer beginning at the right side and put the decimal point to the left of those digits.

Example: 215.7 x 2.4

```
   215.7
  × 2.4
   8628
+ 43140
  51768
```

Because there is one decimal digits in 215.7 and one in 2.4, making a total of two decimal digits, count off 2 places from the right in your answer (51768) and place the decimal point to the left of the last 2 digits: 517.68

If your answer doesn't have enough digits, tack zeroes on to the left of the answer.

Example: $.03 \times .006$

1. Multiply 3 times 6: $3 \times 6 = 18$
2. You need 5 decimal digits in your answer, so tack on 3 zeroes: 00018
3. Put the decimal point at the front of the number (which is 5 digits in from the right): .00018

Practice multiplying decimals:

28. $.05 \times .6$
29. $.053 \times 6.4$
30. $38.1 \times .0184$

DIVIDING DECIMALS

To divide a decimal by a whole number, set up the division $\left(8\overline{)256}\right)$ and immediately bring the decimal point straight up into the answer.

$$\left(8\overline{).256}\right)$$

Then divide as you would normally divide whole numbers.

If you are dividing two decimals, there is an extra step to perform before you can divide. You must first change the problem to one in which you're dividing by a whole number. Move the decimal point to the very right of the number you're dividing by, counting the number of places you're moving it. Then move the decimal point the same number of places to the right in the number you're dividing into.

Example: $.06 \overline{)1.218}$

1. Because there are 2 decimal digits in .06, move the decimal point 2 places to the right in both numbers. Then move the decimal point straight up into the answer:

2. Divide using the new numbers:

$$.06 \overline{)1.21.8}$$

Under certain conditions, you have to tack on zeroes to the right of the last decimal digit in number you're dividing into:

- If there aren't enough digits for you to move the decimal point to the right
- If the answer doesn't come out evenly when you do the division
- If you're dividing a whole number by a decimal. (Then you'll have to tack on the decimal point as well as some zeroes.)

Practice these division problems:

31. $9.8 \div 7$
32. $.0512 \div .0004$
33. $28.6 \div .05$

PERCENTS

A percent is a special kind of fraction, or part of, something. The bottom number (denominator) is always 100. For example, 17% is the same as $\frac{17}{100}$. A percent tells how many out of 100. Thus, 17% means 17 parts out of 100. Because fractions can also be expressed as decimals, 17% is also equivalent to .17, which is 17 hundredths. Sales tax, interest, and discounts are just a few common examples of percents.

CHANGING A DECIMAL TO A PERCENT AND VICE VERSA

To change a decimal to a percent, move the decimal point two places to the right and tack on a percent sign (%) at the end. If the decimal point moves to the very right of the number, you don't have to write the decimal point. If there aren't enough places to move the decimal point, add zeroes on the right before moving the decimal point.

To change a percent to a decimal, drop off the percent sign and move the decimal point two places to the left. If there aren't enough places to move the decimal point, add zeroes on the left before moving the decimal point.

Try changing these decimals to percents:

34. .45
35. .008
36. $.16\frac{2}{3}$

Now change these percents to decimals:

37. 12%
38. $87\frac{1}{2}\%$
39. 250%

CHANGING FRACTIONS TO PERCENTS

To change a fraction to a percent, there are two methods.

Method 1: Multiply the fraction by 100%.
(Note: change 100% to its fractional equivalent before multiplying.)

Example:

Multiply $\frac{1}{4}$ by 100%: $\frac{1}{4} \times \frac{100\%}{1} = \frac{100\%}{4} = 25\%$

Method 2: Divide the fraction's bottom number into the top number; then move the decimal point two places to the right and tack on a percent sign (%).

Divide 4 into 1 and move the decimal point 2 places to the right:

$1 \div 4 = .25 = 25\%$

Try changing these fractions to percents:

40. $\frac{1}{8}$

41. $\frac{13}{25}$

42. $\frac{7}{12}$

CHANGING PERCENTS TO FRACTIONS

To change a percent to a fraction, remove the percent sign and write the number over 100. Then reduce if possible.

Example: Change 4% to a fraction

1. Remove the % and write the fraction 4 over 100: $\frac{4}{100}$

2. Reduce: $\frac{4}{100} = \frac{1}{25}$

Here's a more complicated example: Change $16\frac{2}{3}\%$ to a fraction

1. Remove the % and write the fraction $16\frac{2}{3}$ over 100: $\frac{16\frac{2}{3}}{100}$

2. Since a fraction means "top number divided by bottom number," rewrite the fraction as a division problem: $16\frac{2}{3} \div 100$

3. Change the mixed number ($16\frac{2}{3}$) to an improper fraction ($\frac{50}{3}$): $\frac{50}{3} \div \frac{100}{1}$

4. Flip the second fraction ($\frac{100}{1}$) and multiply $\frac{\cancel{50}^{1}}{3} \times \frac{1}{\cancel{100}_{2}} = \frac{1}{6}$

Now change these percents to fractions:

43. 95%

44. $37\frac{1}{2}\%$

45. 125%

FOR EASY REFERENCE

Sometimes it is more convenient to work with a percentage as a fraction or a decimal. Rather than have to calculate the equivalent fraction or decimal, consider memorizing the equivalence table below. Not only will this increase your efficiency on math tests, it will also be helpful in real-life situations.

DECIMAL	PERCENT (%)	FRACTION
.25	25%	$\frac{1}{4}$
.50	50%	$\frac{1}{2}$
.75	75%	$\frac{3}{4}$
.10	10%	$\frac{1}{10}$
.20	20%	$\frac{2}{10}$
.40	40%	$\frac{4}{10}$
.60	60%	$\frac{6}{10}$
.80	80%	$\frac{8}{10}$
.333	$33\frac{1}{3}\%$	$\frac{1}{3}$
.666	$66\frac{2}{3}\%$	$\frac{2}{3}$

AVERAGES

To calculate an average, you add up the number of items being averaged and divide by the number of items being averaged.

Example: What is the average of 6, 10, and 20?

First, add the three numbers together:
6 + 10 + 20 = 36

Then, divide by 3: 36 ÷ 3 = 12

The average of 6, 10, and 20 is 12.

Shortcut

Here's a good shortcut for some average problems.

- Look at the numbers being averaged. If they are equally spaced, like 5, 10, 15, 20, and 25, then the average is the number in the middle, or 15 in this case.

- If there are an even number of such numbers, say 10, 20, 30, and 40, then there is no middle number. In this case, the average is half way between the two middle numbers. In this case, the average is half way between 20 and 30, or 25.

- If the numbers are almost evenly spaced, you can probably estimate the average without going to the trouble of actually computing it. For example, the average of 10, 20, and 32 is just a little more than 20, the middle number.

Try these average questions:

46. Bob's bowling scores for the last 5 games were 180, 182, 184, 186, and 188. What was his average bowling score?
  a. 182
  b. 183
  c. 184
  d. 185
  e. 186

47. Officer Conroy averaged 30 miles an hour for the two hours he drove in town and 60 miles an hour for the two hours he drove on the highway. What was his average speed in miles per hour?
  a. 18
  b. $22\frac{1}{2}$
  c. 45
  d. 60
  e. 90

48. There are 10 females and 20 males in the first aid course. If the females achieved an average score of 85 and the males achieved an average score of 95, what was the class average? (Hint: don't fall for the trap of taking the average of 85 and 95; there are more 95s being averaged than 85s, so the average is closer to 95.)
  a. $90\frac{2}{3}$
  b. $91\frac{2}{3}$
  c. 92
  d. $92\frac{2}{3}$
  e. 95

ANSWERS

1. $\frac{1}{4}$

2. $\frac{2}{5}$

3. $\frac{3}{8}$

4. 10

5. 6

6. 200

7. $\frac{11}{12}$

8. $\frac{55}{24}$ or $2\frac{7}{24}$

9. $7\frac{1}{4}$

10. $\frac{2}{15}$

11. $\frac{1}{8}$

12. $\frac{19}{12}$ or $1\frac{7}{12}$

13. $\frac{2}{15}$

14. $\frac{8}{35}$

15. $\frac{2}{3}$

16. $\frac{26}{15}$ or $1\frac{11}{15}$

17. 15

18. $\frac{33}{2}$ or $16\frac{1}{2}$

19. $\frac{1}{2}$

20. $5\frac{1}{2}$

21. $\frac{1}{5}$

22. $\frac{5}{1000}$ or $\frac{1}{200}$

23. $3\frac{12}{25}$

24. $123\frac{456}{1000}$ or $123\frac{57}{125}$

25. 4

26. 8.305

27. .907

28. .03

29. .3392

30. .70104

31. 1.4

32. 128

33. 572

34. 45%

35. .8%

36. 16.67%

37. .12

38. .875

39. 2.5

40. 12.5% or $12\frac{1}{2}$%

41. 52%

42. 58.33% or $58\frac{1}{3}$%

43. $\frac{19}{20}$

44. $\frac{3}{8}$

45. $\frac{5}{4}$ or $1\frac{1}{4}$

46. c

47. c

48. b

L·E·S·S·O·N
GEOMETRY AND ALGEBRA
6

Typically, there are very few geometry problems on the math portions of the ASVAB. The problems that are included tend to cover the basics: lines, angles, triangles, rectangles, squares, and circles. You may be asked to find the area or perimeter of a particular shape or the size of an angle. The arithmetic involved is pretty simple, so all you really need are a few definitions and formulas.

USEFUL GEOMETRY TERMS TO KNOW

ANGLE

An angle is formed when two lines (called rays) meet at the same endpoint (called a vertex).

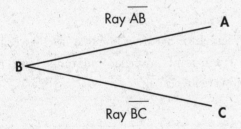

Its symbol is: ∠

There are four types of angles:

- Acute: less than 90°

25°

- Obtuse: more than 90°

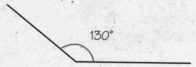

130°

- Right: 90°

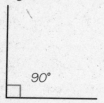

90°

- Straight: 180°

180°

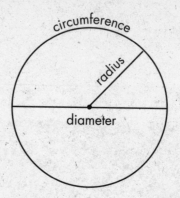

FORMULAS TO KNOW FOR PROBLEMS WITH CIRCLES

Area of a circle: $A = \pi r^2$

Circumference of a circle: $C = 2\pi r$ or πd

Key

π = pi = 3.14

c = circumference

d = diameter

r = radius

CIRCLE

A circle is a continuous curved line. Every point on the curved line is the same distance from the center.

RADIUS

The radius is the line segment from the center to any point on a circle. The radius is half the diameter.

DIAMETER

The diameter is a line through the center of a circle. The diameter is twice the length of the radius.

CIRCUMFERENCE

The circumference is the continuous curved line that forms the circle, the distance around a circle.

LINES

A line is a set of points that extends endlessly in opposite directions.

A line segment is part of a line that lies between two points. These points are called endpoints. The symbol for the line below is $\overline{AB}$.

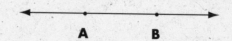

A   **B**

SPECIAL LINE PAIRS

Parallel lines

Parallel lines are lines that never cross each other. They are the same distance apart at all points.

Intersecting Lines

Intersecting Lines are lines that cross each other.

PERPENDICULAR LINES

Perpendicular lines are two lines that intersect in a way that forms a 90° angle.

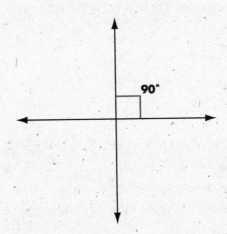

PERIMETER

The perimeter is the distance around a polygon, such as a triangle or a rectangle. The perimeter of a circle is called its circumference.

Perimeter = sum of the lengths of all sides of a polygon

POLYGONS

Polygons are flat figures with three or more connected sides. Triangles, squares, and rectangles are the most common polygons, but polygons can have five, six, seven, and more sides.

RECTANGLE

Four-sided polygon with a right angle and both pairs of opposite sides parallel (which implies that all four angles are right angles and that opposite sides are equal in length):

Area of a rectangle = length × width
Perimeter = (2 × length) + (2 × width)

SQUARE

A square is a rectangle with four equal sides.

Area = (side)^2
Perimeter = 4 × side

TRIANGLE

A triangle is a three-sided polygon. The sides are joined and form three angles.

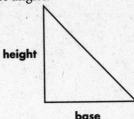

Area $= \frac{1}{2}$(base × height)

Perimeter = sum of the lengths of all 3 sides

Angles: The sum of the three angles of a triangle is always 180°

PRACTICE PROBLEMS IN GEOMETRY

Try your hand at these sample problems similar to those you might see on the ASVAB.

1. What is the area in square inches of a triangle with base 10 and height 8?

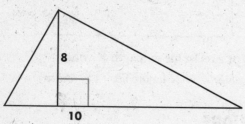

   a. 80
   b. 40
   c. 20
   d. 10
   e. 8

2. Find the perimeter of a triangle with sides of length 3, 4, and 5 units.

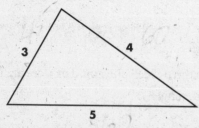

   a. 60 units
   b. 20 units
   c. 12 units
   d. 9 units
   e. 7 units

3. If the area of a square field measures 256 square feet, how many feet of fencing are needed to completely surround the field?

   a. 256
   b. 128
   c. 64
   d. 32
   e. It cannot be determined

4. The length of a rectangle is twice its width. If the perimeter of the rectangle is 30 units, what is the width of the rectangle?

   a. 30
   b. 20
   c. 15
   d. 10
   e. 5

5. A circular opening has a diameter of $8\frac{1}{2}$ inches. What is the radius in inches of a circular disk that will exactly fit into the opening?

   a. 17
   b. 8.5
   c. 8
   d. 4.25
   e. 4

6. The radius of a hoop is 10. If you roll the hoop along a straight path through 6 complete revolutions, approximately how far will it roll, in inches? (Use the value of 3.14 for π)

   a. 31.4
   b. 62.8
   c. 188.4
   d. 376.8
   e. 1884

7. What is the circumference of a round tower whose radius is $3\frac{1}{2}$ feet?

8. The wheel of a bicycle is 26 inches in diameter. If the wheel makes one full turn, how many inches does it travel?

9. A triangular plot has a perimeter of 150 feet. One side of the triangle measures 50 feet. Another side measures 45 feet. What is the length of the third side?

10. Jenny is building a wire fence for her dogs. The area that she is fencing is 7 feet wide and 8 feet long. How many feet of wire fencing will she need, at the very least?

Use the picture below to answer questions 11 and 12.

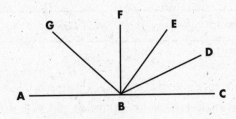

11. Which of the following angles is acute?
   a. ∠ABF
   b. ∠ABE
   c. ∠EBD

12. Which of the following angles is obtuse?
   a. ∠GBC
   b. ∠FBE
   c. ∠FBC

ALGEBRA

Algebra questions do not appear on every ASVAB. However, when they do, they typically cover the mate-rial you learned in pre-algebra or in the first few months of a high school algebra course. Algebra is a way to express and solve problems using numbers and symbols. These symbols, called unknowns or variables, are letters of the alphabet that are used to represent numbers.

For example, let's say you're asked to find out what number, when added to 3, gives you a total of 5. Using algebra, you could express the problem as $x + 3 = 5$. The variable x represents the number you're trying to find.

Here's another example, but this one uses only variables. To find the distance traveled, multiply the rate of travel (speed) by the amount of time traveled: $d = r \times t$. The variable d stands for distance, r stands for rate, and t stands for time.

In algebra, the variables may take on different val-ues. In other words, they vary, and that's why they're called variables.

OPERATIONS

Algebra uses the same operations as arithmetic: addi-tion, subtraction, multiplication, and division. In arith-metic, we might say $3 + 4 = 7$, while in algebra we would talk about two numbers whose values we don't know that add up to 7, or $x + y = 7$.

Here's how each operation translates to algebra:

Algebraic Operations	
The sum of two numbers	$x + y$
The difference of two numbers	$x - y$
The product of two numbers	$x \times y$ or $x \cdot y$ or xy
The quotient of two numbers	$\frac{x}{y}$

EQUATIONS

An equation is a mathematical sentence stating that two quantities are equal. For example:

$$2x = 10$$
$$x + 5 = 8$$

The idea is to find a replacement for the unknown that will make the sentence true. That's called solving the equation. Thus, in the first example, $x = 5$ because $2 \times 5 = 10$. In the second example, $x = 3$ because $3 + 5 = 8$.

Sometimes you can solve an equation by inspection, as with the above examples. Other equations may be more complicated and require a step-by-step solution, for example:

$$\frac{n+2}{4} + 1 = 3$$

The general approach is to consider an equation like a balance scale, with both sides equally balanced. Essentially, whatever you do to one side, you must also do to the other side to maintain the balance. Thus, if you were to add 2 to the left side, you'd also have to add 2 to the right side.

Let's apply this balance concept to our complicated equation above. Remembering that we want to solve it for n, we must somehow rearrange it so the n is isolated on one side of the equation. Its value will then be on the other side. Looking at the equation, you can see that n has been increased by 2 and then divided by 4 and ultimately added to 1. Therefore, we'll undo these operations to isolate n.

Begin by subtracting 1 from both sides of the equation:
$$\frac{n+2}{4} + 1 = 3$$
$$\phantom{\frac{n+2}{4}}\ -1\ -1$$
$$\frac{n+2}{4} = 2$$

Next multiply both sides by 4:
$$\cancel{4} \times \frac{n+2}{\cancel{4}} = 2 \times 4$$
$$n + 2 = 8$$

Finally, subtract 2 from both sides:
$$n + 2 = 8$$
$$\ -2\ -2$$
Which isolates n and solves the equation:
$$n = 6$$

Notice that each operation in the original equation was undone by multiplication. In general, each operation can be undone by its inverse:

Algebraic Inverses	
OPERATION	INVERSE
Addition	Subtraction
Subtraction	Addition
Multiplication	Division
Division	Multiplication

After you solve an equation, check your work by plugging the answer back into the original equation to make sure it balances

Solve each equation:

_____ **13.** $x + 5 = 12$

_____ **14.** $3x + 6 = 18$

_____ **15.** $\frac{x}{4} = 7$

POSITIVE AND NEGATIVE NUMBERS

Positive and negative numbers, also known as signed numbers, are best shown as points along the number line:

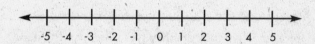

Numbers to the left of 0 are *negative* and those to the right are *positive*. Zero is neither negative nor positive. If a number is written without a sign, it is assumed to be positive. Notice that when you are on the negative side of then number line, numbers with bigger values are actually smaller. For example, -5 is *less than* -2. You come into contact with negative numbers more often than you might think; for example, very cold temperatures are recoded as negative numbers.

As you move to the right along the number line, the numbers get larger. Mathematically, to indicate that one number, say 4, is *greater than* another number, say -2, the *greater than* sign ($>$) is used: $4 > -2$

On the other hand, to say that -2 is *less than* 4, we use the *less than* sign ($<$): $-2 < 4$

ARITHMETIC WITH POSITIVE AND NEGATIVE NUMBERS

The following table lists rules for doing arithmetic with signed numbers. Notice that when a negative number follows an operation it is enclosed in parentheses to avoid confusion.

RULE	EXAMPLE
Addition	
If both numbers have the same sign, just add them. The answer has the same sign as the numbers being added.	$3+5 = 8$ $-3 + (-5) = -8$
If both numbers have different signs, subtract the smaller number from the larger. The answer has the same sign as the larger number.	$-3 + 5 = 2$ $3 + (-5) = -2$
If both numbers are the same but have opposite signs, the sum is zero.	$3 + (-3) = 0$
Subtraction	
Change the sign of the number to be subtracted and then add as above.	$3 - 5 = 3 + (-5) = -2$ $-3 - 5 = -3 + (-5)$
Multiplication	
Multiply the numbers together. If both number have the same sign, the answer is positive; otherwise it is negative.	$3 \times 5 = 15$ $-3 \times (-5) = 15$ $-3 \times 5 = -15$ $3 \times -5 = -15$
If one number is zero, the answer is zero	$3 \times 0 = 0$
Division	
Divide the numbers. If both numbers have the same sign, the answer is positive; otherwise it is negative.	$15 \div 3 = 5$ $-15 \div (-3) = 5$ $-15 \div 3 = -5$ $15 \div (-3) = -5$
If the number being divided (the dividend) is zero, the answer is zero	$0 \div 3 = 0$

When more than one arithmetic operations appear, you must know the correct sequence in which to perform the operations. For example, do you know what to do first to calculate $2 + 3 \times 4$? You're right if you said "multiply first." The correct answer is 14. If you add first, you'll get the wrong answer of 20. The correct order in which to do things (or order of operations) is:

1. parentheses
2. exponents
3. multiplication
4. division
5. addition
6. subtraction

If you remember this saying (mnemonic device), you'll know the order of operations: **P**lease **E**xcuse **M**y **D**ear **A**unt **S**ally.

Even when signed numbers appear in an equation, the step-by-step solution works exactly as it does for positive numbers. You just have to remember the arithmetic rules for negative numbers. For example, let's solve $-14x + 2 = -5$

1. Subtract from both sides:

$$-14x + 2 = -5$$
$$\underline{\quad -2 \quad -2}$$

2. Divide both sides by -14:

$$\frac{-14x}{-14} = \frac{-7}{-14}$$
$$x = \frac{1}{2}$$

Now try these problems:

16. $1 - 3\,x\,(-4) = x$

17. $-3x + 6 = -18$

18. $\frac{x}{-4} + 3 = -7$

ALGEBRAIC EXPRESSIONS

An algebraic expression is a group of numbers, unknowns, and arithmetic operations, like: $3x - 2y$. This one may be translated as three times some number minus two times another number. To evaluate an algebraic expression, replace each variable with its value. For example, if $x = 5$ and $y = 4$, we would evaluate $3x - 2y$ as the following:

$$3(5) - 2(4) = 15 - 8 = 7$$

Evaluate these expressions by plugging in the given values:

19. $4a + 3b$; $a = 2$ and $b = -1$

20. $3mn - 4m + 2n$; $m = 3$ and $n = -3$

21. $-2x - \frac{y}{2} + 4z$; $x = 5$ and $y = -4$ and $z = 6$

ANSWERS

1. b
2. c
3. c
4. e
5. d
6. d
7. 21.98 feet
8. 81.64 inches
9. 55 feet
10. 30 feet
11. c
12. a
13. 7
14. 4
15. 28
16. 13
17. 8
18. 40
19. 5
20. −45
21. 16

L · E · S · S · O · N
WORD PROBLEMS
7

A word problem tells a story. It may present a situation with numbers and/or unknown information (also called a *variable*). Your job is to translate that word problem into a math problem to solve. Many of the math problems on the ASVAB are word problems. A word problem can include any kind of math, including simple arithmetic, fractions, decimals, percentages—even algebra and geometry. This chapter will give you some helpful hints to use when you try to solve word problems.

STEPS TO SOLVING WORD PROBLEMS

Some simple word problems can be solved by common sense. Most word problems, however, require several steps. Here are some steps to help you solve word problems:

1. **Read a word problem in chunks, rather than straight through.** As you read each chunk, stop to think about what it means. To represent that chunk, take notes, draw a diagram, draw a picture, or write an equation. You may even want to underline important information in each chunk. Repeat this process with each chunk. Reading a word problem in sections makes the problem easier to understand. Also, you probably won't have to read it again to answer it.

2. **Make a plan of attack.** Figure out what information you already have. Then think about how you're going to use it to solve the problem.

3. **Reread the question** to make sure you've answered the right question after you get your answer. This will help you avoid the careless mistake of answering the wrong question.

4. **Check your work after you get an answer.** In a multiple-choice test, don't assume your answer is correct just because it matches one of the answers given. The most common mistakes are often included in the answer choices. You should always check your work if you have time. Here are a few suggestions:

- Ask yourself if the answer is reasonable: Does it make sense?
- Plug your answer back into the problem: Does it hold together?
- Work the problem a second time, using a different method if you can.
- If a question stumps you, try working the problem backwards.

TRANSLATING WORD PROBLEMS

The hardest part of any word problem is translating the story into math. When you read a problem, sometimes you can translate it word for word from English statements into mathematical statements. For many problems, you will write out an equation. An equation is a number sentence that shows two parts that are equal: $45 + 12 = 57$ is a number sentence *and* an equation.

An equation may involve an unknown amount. The unknown is a way of saying that you don't know that part of the equation. Sometimes this unknown amount is represented by a letter. For example, suppose you went shopping and bought a sweater for $45. You also bought a pair of gloves, but you can't remember how much they cost. You do remember that you spent $57 in all. The amount of the gloves is the unknown. You use the letter x to represent the price of the gloves. The equation looks like this: $45 + x = 57$. When you solve the problem you learn that $x = 12$. The gloves cost $12.

Often, key words in the problem hint at the mathematical operation to be performed and how to translate that story into math. Think of the key word as a word to look for in a word problem that will signal to you what operation to use to set up the equation and solve the problem. Here are some translation tips:

Equals   Key words: is, are, has

English	Math
Judi **has** 5 books.	$J = 5$
Bob **is** 18 years old.	$B = 18$
There **are** 7 hats.	$H = 7$

Addition   Key words: sum; more, greater, or older than; total; altogether

English	Math
The **sum** of two numbers is 10.	$X + Y = 10$
Karen has $5 **more** than Sam.	$K = 5 + S$
Judi is 2 years **older** than Tony.	$J = 2 + T$
The **total** of three numbers is 25.	$A + B + C = 25$
The base is 3" **greater than** the height.	$B = 3 + H$
How much do Joan and Tom have **altogether**?	$J + T = ?$

Subtraction   Key words: difference, less or younger than, remain, left over

English	Math
Jay is 2 years **younger** than Brett.	$J = B - 2$
After Carol ate 3 apples, R apples **remained**.	$R = A - 3$
The **difference** between two numbers is 17.	$X + Y = 17$
Mike has 5 **less** cats than twice the number Jan has.	$M = 2J - 5$

Multiplication   Key words: of, product, times

English	Math
Half **of** the boys	$\frac{1}{2} \times B$
The **product** of two numbers is 12.	$A \times B = 12$
20% **of** Matthew's baseball caps	$.20 \times M$

Division   Key word: per

English	Math
22 miles **per** gallon	22 miles/gallon
15 drops **per** teaspoon	15 drops/teaspoon

Distance Formula: distance = rate x time
Key words are movement words like: plane, train, boat, car, walk, run, climb, swim, and also how far, how long

How far did the plane travel in 4 hours if it averaged 300 miles per hour?	$D = 300 \times 4$ $D = 1200$ miles
Ben walked 20 miles in 4 hours. What was his average **speed**?	$20 = r \times 4$ 5 miles per hour $= r$

SOLVING WORD PROBLEMS USING THE TRANSLATION TABLE

Now let's try to solve the following problem using our translation rules.

EXAMPLE

Carla is reading a novel that has a total of 336 pages. On Friday, she read 35 pages. On Saturday, she read twice the number of pages she read on Friday. How many more pages does she have left to read?

a. 105
b. 231
c. 266
d. 301

Here's how we marked up the question. Notice how we underlined key phrases and we used letters to represent words: *t* for total, *F* instead of Friday, and *S* instead of Saturday.

Carla is reading a novel that has a total of 336 pages. On Friday, she read 35 pages. On Saturday, she read twice the number of pages she read on Friday. How many more pages does she have left to read?

$t = 336$
$F = 35$
$S = 2 \times 35$
$? = left$

The words *more* and *left* hint at both addition and subtraction. The word *twice* (meaning 2 times more) hints at multiplication.

What we know:

- Carla read 35 pages one day.
- Carla read 2 times 35 pages the next day.
- The book has a total of 336 pages.

The question itself: How many more pages does she have left to read?

Plan of attack:

- Find the number of pages she has already read.
- Find out how many pages are left.

SOLUTION

You know how many pages Carla read on Friday: 35. If you want to find out how many pages she read on Saturday, you will use multiplication: $2 \times 35 = 70$. Next, you will use addition to find out how many pages she has already read: $35 + 70 = 105$. But the question asks, "How many pages does she have left to read?" The word *left* indicates that you will use subtraction: $366 - 105 = 231$. So to answer this question, you must take three steps.

You must use three operations: addition, subtraction, and multiplication

Step 1: $2 \times 35 = 70$
Step 2: $35 + 70 = 105$
Step 3: $366 - 105 = 231$
Answer: Carla has 231 pages left to read.

CHECK YOUR WORK

Check your work by plugging your answer back into the original problem. See if the whole thing makes sense:

Carla is reading a novel that has a total of 336 pages. On Friday, she read 35 pages. On Saturday, she read 70 pages. She has 231 pages left to read.

Carla has already read 105 pages (25 + 70). If she reads 231 more (105 + 231 = 336), she will have read all 336 pages.

PRACTICE WORD PROBLEMS

Practice using the translation table to help you solve problems that require you to work with basic arithmetic. Answers are at the end of the chapter.

1. Joan went shopping with $100 and returned home with only $18.42. How much money did she spend?
   a. $81.58
   b. $72.68
   c. $72.58
   d. $71.68
   e. $71.58

2. Mark invited ten friends to a party. Each friend brought three guests. How many people came to the party, excluding Mark?
   a. 3
   b. 10
   c. 30
   d. 40
   e. 41

3. The office secretary can type 80 words per minute on his word processor. How many minutes will it take him to type a report containing 760 words?
   a. 8
   b. 8.5
   c. 9
   d. 9.5
   e. 10

4. Mr. Wallace is writing a budget request to upgrade his personal computer system. He wants to purchase 4mb of RAM, which will cost $100, two new software programs at $350 each, a tape backup system for $249, and an additional tape for $25. What is the total amount Mr. Wallace should write on his budget request?
   a. $724
   b. $974
   c. $1049
   d. $1064
   e. $1074

FRACTIONS

5. The length of a table plus $\frac{1}{5}$ of its length is 35 inches. How long is the table, in inches?
   a. 30
   b. 40
   c. 42
   d. 45

6. An outside wall is $5\frac{7}{8}$ inches thick. The wall consists of $\frac{1}{2}$ inch of drywall and $3\frac{3}{4}$ inches of insulation, and $\frac{5}{8}$ inch of wall sheathing. The remaining thickness is siding. How thick is the siding?
   a. $\frac{1}{8}$ inch
   b. $\frac{1}{4}$ inch
   c. $\frac{1}{2}$ inch
   d. 1 inch

7. A certain test is scored by adding 1 point for each correct answer and subtracting $\frac{1}{4}$ of a point for each incorrect answer. If Jan answered 31 questions correctly and 9 questions incorrectly, what was her score?

   a. $28\frac{3}{4}$

   b. $28\frac{1}{4}$

   c. 26

   d. $22\frac{1}{4}$

8. Bart took a taxi $\frac{1}{4}$ of the distance to Mandy's house. He took a bus for $\frac{1}{3}$ of the distance to her house. Finally, he walked the remaining 5 miles to her house. How many miles did Bart travel in all?

   a. 9

   b. 10

   c. $11\frac{3}{4}$

   d. 12

9. Ursula can run $3\frac{1}{2}$ miles per hour. If she runs for $2\frac{1}{4}$ hours, how far will she run, in miles?

   a. $5\frac{3}{4}$

   b. $6\frac{1}{4}$

   c. $7\frac{7}{8}$

   d. 18

DECIMALS

10. At a certain discount store, if you purchase 5 pairs of socks, you get one pair of socks free. If one pair of socks costs $1.25, and Jeff left the store with 18 pairs of socks, how much did he spend?

    a. $18.75

    b. 20.00

    c. $21.25

    d. $22.50

11. Roland has a stack of small boxes, all the same size. If the stack measures 55.5 centimeters high and each box is 9.25 centimeters high, how many boxes does he have?

    a. 5

    b. 6

    c. 7

    d. 8

12. Selma bought four items at the grocery store that cost $1.98, $2.65, $4.29, and $6.78. She gave the clerk a $20 bill. How much change did she receive?

    a. $3.30

    b. $4.30

    c. $4.40

    d. $15.70

13. At a price of $ .82 per pound, which of the following comes closest to the cost of a turkey weighing $9\frac{1}{4}$ pounds?

    a. $6.80

    b. $7.00

    c. $7.60

    d. $8.20

PERCENTS

14. If the price of a bottle of maple syrup is reduced from $4 to $3, by what percent is the price reduced?

a. $\frac{1}{4}$ %

b. $\frac{1}{3}$ %

c. 1%

d. 25%

15. A certain credit card company charges $12\frac{1}{4}$% interest on the unpaid balance. If Mona has an unpaid balance of $220, how much interest will she be charged for one month?

a. $2.75

b. $14.4

c. $24.00

d. $26.95

16. Fifteen percent of the 3,820 employees at TechnoCorps were hired this year. How many of TechnoCorps employees were NOT hired this year?

a. 573

b. 1,910

c. 3,247

d. 3,805

17. Gilbert won 12 out of the 19 tennis matches he played in. What percent of his matches did he lose, rounded to the nearest percent?

a. 37%

b. 39%

c. 59%

d. 63%

ANSWERS

1. a
2. d
3. d
4. e
5. a
6. d
7. a
8. d
9. c
10. a
11. b
12. b
13. c
14. d
15. d
16. c
17. a

S · E · C · T · I · O · N

3

READING COMPREHENSION FOR THE PARAGRAPH COMPREHENSION SUBTEST

Because reading is such a vital skill, the Armed Services Vocational Aptitude Battery includes a reading comprehension section that tests your ability to understand what you read. The tips and exercises in this section will help you improve your comprehension of written passages so that you can increase your score in this area. Understanding written materials is part of almost any job. That's why the ASVAB attempts to measure how well applicants understand what they read. Memos, policies, procedures, reports—these are all things you'll be expected to understand if you enlist in the armed services.

The Paragraph Comprehension subtest of the ASVAB is in a multiple-choice format and asks questions based on brief passages, much like the standardized tests that students take in school. Almost all standardized test questions test your reading skills. After all, you can't answer the question if you can't read it. Similarly, you can't study your training materials or learn new procedures once you're on the job if you can't read well. So reading comprehension is vital not only on the test but also for the rest of your career.

ACTIVE READING

Good readers are active readers. They see reading as an involved process. That's why they understand so much of what they read. To be an active reader you should:

1. **Write when you read.** Writing while you read can really help you absorb information better. Try to
   - **Underline key words and ideas** to help important information stand out so that you can remember it later and summarize it.
   - **Circle and look up unfamiliar words and phrases**—you need to know what all the words in a sentence mean in order to completely understand what someone is saying.
   - **List any questions and comments you might have.** As you read, you're bound to have questions. You're likely to have reactions to the reading as well. Writing down your questions and thoughts makes you think about what you read, and that means you will understand the material better.

2. **Think like a detective when you read.** Pay careful attention to the details in sentences and passages to find clues that help you understand the writer's ideas better. Making observations and finding these clues is essential because your observations are what lead you to logical inferences about what you read. Inferences are conclusions based on reason,

fact, or evidence. If you misunderstand what you read, it is often because you haven't looked closely enough at the text.

TYPES OF READING COMPREHENSION QUESTIONS

You have probably encountered reading comprehension questions before, where you are given a passage to read and then have to answer multiple-choice questions about it. This kind of question has an advantage for you as a test taker: You don't have to know anything about the topic of the passage because you're being tested only on the information the passage provides.

The disadvantage is that you have to know where and how to find that information quickly in an unfamiliar text. This makes it easy to fall for one of the wrong answer choices, especially since they're designed to mislead you.

The best way to do well on this passage/question format is to be very familiar with the kinds of questions that are typically asked on the test. Questions most frequently ask you to:

1. identify a specific fact or detail in the passage
2. uncover the main idea of the passage
3. make an inference based on the passage
4. define a vocabulary word from the passage

The following list of important words to know—words that will help you become a better, more active reader who understands what he or she reads—will greatly help you in your quest to answer reading comprehension questions.

WORDS EVERY GOOD READER SHOULD KNOW

Argument	a discussion aimed a proving something to be true; a claim supported by reasons or evidence
Basic Information	core facts or data, essential knowledge or ideas
Cause	a person or thing that makes something happen or creates an effect
Chronology	the order in which things happen
Compare	to examine in order to find similarities between two or more items
Conclusion	belief or opinion based on reasoning
Connotation	the suggested or implied meaning of a word; its emotional impact
Context	the words and ideas surrounding a word that help give it its meaning
Contrast	to show the differences between two or more items
Effect	a change created by an action or cause
Emotional	drawn from the emotions; based on strong mental feelings
Fact	something known for certain to be true
Formality	the quality of being proper, ceremonious
General	broad, wide, nonspecific; applying to most or all
Imply	to hint or suggest without stating directly
Indifferent	uncaring, showing no interest
Logical	according to reason; based on evidence or good common sense
Main Idea	the thought that holds a passage together
Narrator	the person who tells the story
Objective	unaffected by the thoughts, feelings, and experiences of the writer
Observant	paying careful attention
Observation	something seen or noticed
Opinion	something believed to be true
Point of View	the person or position through which you see things
Rank	position or value in relation to other in a group
Reason	a motive or grounds for something; good sense or judgment
Sentence Structure	the size and parts of a sentence
Specific	particular, exact
Style	the way of doing something, such as writing, speaking, or dressing; the manner in which something is done
Subject	whom or what the passage is about
Subjective	based on the thoughts, feelings, and experiences of the writer
Tone	the mood or attitude conveyed by words or speech
Topic Sentence	the sentence that states the main idea
Transitions	words and phrases that link ideas and how the ideas relate to each other
Unfamiliar	something you don't know

L · E · S · S · O · N

THE BASICS

8

This lesson will help you learn how to become a good active reader. You will master a few basic skills to build a strong reading foundation. By the end of this lesson (and with a little practice) you should be able to:

1. uncover the basic facts in a passage
2. find the main idea of a passage
3. figure out what words mean without a dictionary
4. tell the difference between fact and opinion

GETTING THE BASIC INFORMATION

The first thing you need to do when you read anything is get the basic information. This includes the who, the what, the when, the where, the how, and the why. What does the passage tell you? What happens? To whom? When? Where? How? Why?

The questions you will ask yourself will change from reading to reading, but the idea is always the same: You need to find the basic information. Being observant while you read will help you find this information.

The following is a short paragraph that could be from a local newspaper article. Read it carefully and actively. As you read, look for the basic facts and think about the who, what, when, where, why, and how.

Yesterday the house of Mr. and Mrs. Jason White was robbed. The thieves entered the house at 13 Elm Avenue around noon. Mr. White and his wife, Alison, were not home. The house had an expensive security system linked to the local police station. But no alarms went off at the precinct. The robbery wasn't discovered until Mrs. White came home at 3:45 PM Police say that the thieves disconnected the security system. The thieves stole all of the Whites's furniture, jewelry, office equipment, and artwork. Mrs. White is an art appraiser. She values the stolen property at $1.6 million.

Reading actively should help you find the basic information in this passage. Here are some questions you could ask to find the facts:

1. What happened?
2. When did it happen?
3. Where did it happen?
4. How did it happen?

5. Who discovered the theft?
6. When was the theft discovered?
7. What was stolen?
8. How much is the stolen property worth?

Here's how this passage might look after an active reading. The basic facts have been underlined. There are notes in the margins. There is also a definition for appraiser.

when   who   what happened—robbery

Yesterday the house of <u>Mr. & Mrs. Jason White</u> was <u>robbed.</u> The thieves entered the house at <u>13 Elm Avenue</u> around noon. Mr. White and his wife, Alison, were not home. The house had an expensive security system linked to the local police station. But no alarms went off at the precinct. The robbery wasn't discovered until Mrs. White came home at 3:45 PM. Police say that <u>the thieves disconnected the security system.</u> The thieves stole all of the Whites's <u>furniture, jewelry, office equipment, and artwork.</u> Mrs. White is an art appraiser. She values the stolen property at <u>$1.6 million.</u>

how

what was taken

noon–3:45 = time gap between robbery & discovery

The thieves picked a good target!

appraise: to estimate the value or quality of

Here are the answers to the questions:
1. What happened? *The White's house was robbed.*
2. When did it happen? *Yesterday*
3. Where did it happen? *13 Elm Avenue*
4. How did it happen? *The thieves disconnected the security system.*
5. Who discovered the theft? *Mrs. White*
6. When was the theft discovered? *At 3:45 in the afternoon*
7. What was stolen? *Their furniture, jewelry, office equipment, and artwork*
8. How much is the stolen property worth? *$1.6 million*

This is the basic information in the paragraph. You could ask more questions and there is no rule to tell you how many questions you should ask yourself. What you need to know depends on what kind of text you're reading. Are you reading a magazine article for pleasure about an athlete? Then just a handful of questions should do. But, if it's a chapter in a history book, or a passage on the ASVAB, it has important information that you'll need to understand and remember. So in this case, you'll need to ask yourself more questions.

PRACTICE 1

In the following practice exercise, read the passage below carefully and actively. Then answer the questions that follow.

Remember to be an active reader. Circle and look up any unfamiliar words, underline key words and ideas, and write questions and comments in the margins. Ask yourself questions as you read. When you are done, you can check your answers at the end of the lesson.

> The U.S. Postal Service is more efficient than ever. Mail used to take months to arrive. It was delivered by horse or by foot. Now trucks, trains, and planes move it around the country in days or hours. First class mail arrives in three days or less. Urgent mail can move even faster. Priority Mail is guaranteed to go anywhere in the U.S. in three days or less. Express Mail will get your package there overnight.

Questions

1. Who or what is this passage about?
2. How was mail delivered in the past?
3. How is mail delivered now?
4. How long does first class mail take?
5. How long does Priority Mail take?
6. How long does Express Mail take?

FINDING THE MAIN IDEA

The main idea is the thought that holds the passage together. The *why* of the passage. A good reader asks himself, "Why did he author write this? What idea does he or she want me to accept?" Asking yourself these questions will help lead you to the main idea of a passage.

SUBJECT OR MAIN IDEA

People often confuse the subject with the main idea. But there's an important difference. To see the difference, take another look at the passage about the postal system.

> The U.S. Postal Service is more efficient than ever. Mail used to take months to arrive. It was delivered by horse or by foot. Now trucks, trains, and planes move it around the country in days or hours. First class mail arrives in three days or less. Urgent mail can move even faster. Priority Mail is guaranteed to go anywhere in the U.S. in three days or less. Express Mail will get your package there overnight.

Reading tests often ask, "What is the main idea of this passage?" For the passage above, you might answer, "the post office." But you'd be making a common mistake. The passage is *about* the post office, but the post office is not the main idea. Instead, the post office is the subject of the passage. The subject is who or what the passage is about. The main idea, on the other hand, says something about the subject.

For example, say the subject of a passage is ice cream. The main idea might be that chocolate is the most popular flavor of ice cream. This claim, like most main ideas, needs some proof or support. Writers provide lots of support for the main idea.

Now look back at the paragraph about the postal service. The subject is the post office. Now see if you can find the main idea. Read the passage carefully again and look for the idea that makes a claim about the subject. Remember, the idea should be general and it should hold together the whole paragraph. Answer the following question:

Which sentence best summarizes the main idea of the passage?

a. Express Mail is a good way to send urgent mail.

b. Mail service today is very effective.

c. First class mail usually takes three days or less.

All three options make a claim about mail services, But answers *a* and *c* are too specific to be the main idea. Neither of these answer choices covers all of the ideas in the paragraph.

Only answer choice *b* is general enough to cover the whole paragraph. All of the other sentences support the idea in answer choice *b*. Each sentence offers proof for that idea. The writer's motive is to show that the post office is better than ever. That main idea is stated in the first sentence, and the rest of the sentences support that idea.

The main idea of a passage, then, makes a claim about its subject. But the main idea does more that that. It also holds the whole passage together. All of the other sentences in the passage must have something to do with that idea. They usually give specific examples or expla-nations. In a way, the main idea is like a net over the passage. It is the general idea that covers all of the specific ideas in the paragraph.

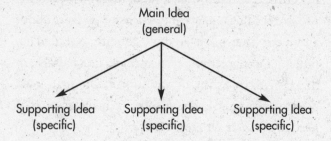

The main idea is both a claim about a subject and the general idea that holds together all of the ideas in the passage.

TOPIC SENTENCES

The topic sentence is a claim about the subject. It is usually a claim that needs support or proof. Remember that a topic sentence clearly states the main idea. It must be general enough to cover all of the ideas in the passage. It also makes a claim about the subject.

PRACTICE 2

Look at the following paragraph. Read it carefully and then underline the sentence that best states the main idea. You can check your answer at the end of the lesson.

Erik always played cops and robber when he was a boy. Now he's a police officer. Lauren always played school as a little girl. Today she's a math teacher. Kara always played store. Now she owns her own clothing store. Some lucky people have always known what they want to do with their lives.

INTRODUCING SPECIFIC EXAMPLES

Readers need to see that the claim made in the topic sentence is true and that's what the other supporting sentences in the postal service paragraph do. They show readers that the postal service is more efficient than ever.

Supporting sentences often begin with signal words that tell you they are about to introduce specific example. Sentences that begin with these words and phrases are usually not topic sentences, but rather they are supporting sentences, introducing specific examples. Here are some words and phrases that often introduce specific examples.

for example	furthermore	in addition
in particular	some	others
for instance		

Sometimes you might have trouble finding the main idea. You can try crossing out sentences that begin with these words. Then you'll have fewer sentences to choose from. The topic sentences should be easier to find.

DEFINING WORDS IN CONTEXT

As you read, you will often see unfamiliar words, or words you don't know the meanings of. You might have a dictionary. Then you can look up those words. But what if you don't have a dictionary? How can you understand what you're reading if you don't know what the words mean?

You can often figure out what a word means if you look at its context—the words and ideas surrounding a word that help give it its meaning. Reading comprehension tests, like the one on the ASVAB, often test your ability to find the meaning of words based on the context of the passage.

FINDING MEANING IN CONTEXT

Sometimes you can't understand an entire sentence, or group of sentences, if you don't understand one key word. For example, look at the following sentence.

The new policy will *substantially* cut employee benefits.

Can you fully understand the sentence without knowing what *substantially* means? As an employee, you will want to know what *substantially* means. How much will your benefits be cut? This is an important question. Is *substantially* a little or a lot? There aren't enough clues in this sentence; to figure out what the word means, you need more context.

Here's the same sentence in a paragraph.

The new policy will substantially cut employee benefits. Employees will lose their dental coverage. Regular doctor check-ups will no longer be covered. And psychiatric coverage will be cut from six visits to two.

You should be able to figure out what *substantially* means now.

Substantially means:
a. just barely
b. a little, but not too much
c. small
d. a lot

The answer is *d* a lot. The paragraph describes a big cut in coverage. Both dental care and regular check-ups will no longer be covered and psychiatric care will be cut by two-thirds. These are serious cutbacks. You may have also noticed that *substantially* is similar to the word *substance*. Something that has substance is weighty or solid. It is not light. Your knowledge of related words can also help you define words in context.

PRACTICE 3

Read the sentences below carefully. Use context to find out what the italicized words mean. Then circle the correct meanings. Check your answers at the end of the lesson.

1. I accidentally told Nell about her surprise party. What a stupid *blunder*!
   A *blunder* is
   a. a jerk
   b. an idea
   c. a mistake
   d. a get-together

2. Our successful salespeople share one personality *trait*: honesty.
   A *trait* is
   a. a feature or aspect
   b. a problem or disorder
   c. a difference
   d. a similarity

3. Please return the pink copy. *Retain* the yellow copy for your records.
   To *retain* means
   a. to copy
   b. to throw away
   c. to read
   d. to keep

PRACTICE 4

Provide context for the words below. Write a sentence or two for each word. The sentences should show the reader what the words mean. Check your answers at the end of the lesson.

Example:

word: glimpse
meaning: to catch a quick view of
context: I'm not sure what he looked like. I only glimpsed the man's face before he disappeared around the corner.

1. word: mundane
   meaning: dull, boring, routine
   context:

2. word: teem
   meaning: to be full of, to be present in large numbers
   context:

THE DIFFERENCE BETWEEN FACT AND OPINION

Sometimes people tell you what they *know* is true—they are telling you facts. Other times they tell you what they *think* is true—they are telling you opinions.

A fact is

- something *known* for certain to have happened
- something *known* for certain to be true
- something *known* for certain to exist

An opinion, on the other hand, is

- something *believed* to have happened
- something *believed* to be true
- something *believed* to exist

The key difference between fact and opinion is the difference between *knowing* and *believing*. Opinions are often based on facts, but opinions are still what people think or feel. They're not what people know. You can argue about an opinion, but you can't argue about a fact. In other words, opinions are debatable while facts are not.

USING FACTS TO SUPPORT OPINIONS

People can have opinions about almost anything. What's important is that they support their opinions. An opinion supported by facts is a reasonable opinion. In fact, that's mostly what you read about. Writers make a claim about their subject and that claim is often an opinion. Then they offer facts to support their opinion.

Think about your own opinions. You could write a topic sentence about your friend Margarita:

Margarita is a good friend.

This is a good topic sentence. It makes a claim about its subject, Margarita, and it's also an opinion. It is something you could argue about. After all, someone could make an opposite claim:

Margarita is a bad friend.

This is another good topic sentence. It's also another opinion. A good writer will now show readers that this is a reasonable opinion. How? By offering supporting facts.

Margarita is a good friend. She always asks me how I am. If I have a problem, she is always willing to listen to me talk about it. For my last birthday, she organized a surprise party for me and invited all my friends. She even baked me a birthday cake.

The topic sentences states an opinion and the rest of the sentences support that opinion. They offer facts about Margarita. This makes it an effective paragraph. Now, here is a writer who doesn't support his opinion well.

Margarita is a bad friend. I don't think that her jokes are funny, and she doesn't seem to care about me at all. And, she has stupid ideas about politics.

The first paragraph about Margarita is much better because it's not just an opinion. It's opinion supported by fact. The second paragraph is all opinion. Every sentence is arguable and the sentences show what the author *thinks* is true, not what is *known* to be true. The second paragraph doesn't include specific facts to show why Margarita is a bad friend, it includes only what the author *thinks* about Margarita.

PRACTICE 5

Read the following claims carefully. Are they fact or opinion? Write an F in the blank if the claim is a fact and an O in the blank if the claim is an opinion. When you are done, you can check your answers at the end of the lesson.

1. _____The Olympics are held every two years.
2. _____The Olympics are fun to watch.

3. _____ The Olympics should be held every year.

4. _____ The 1996 Summer Olympics were held in Atlanta, Georgia.

5. _____ The long jump is the most exciting Olympic Event.

REVIEW

So far you know how to get the basic information from a passage. You know that asking the who, what, when, where, why, and how will help you gather important information from what you are reading. You can also tell the difference between the main idea and the subject of a passage. You know that the main idea makes a claim about the subject and is general enough to hold the passage together. The other sentences in the passage all support the main idea, which is often expressed in a topic sentence. In addition, you know how to figure out what words mean from the context. You also know how to look for clues in the words and sentences around unfamiliar words. Finally, you learned that a fact is something *known* to be true. While an opinion is something *believed* to be true. Many main ideas are opinions. Good writers use facts to support their opinions.

REVIEW PRACTICE

Now you can put all the skills you just learned together by reading this longer passage. Read the following passage and answer the questions. Check your answers at the end of the lesson.

Bicycles

Today, bicycles are so common that it's hard to believe they haven't always been around. But two hundred years ago, bicycles didn't even exist, and the first bicycle, invented in Germany in 1818, was nothing like our bicycles today. It was made of wood and didn't even have pedals. Since then, however, numerous innovations and improvements in design have made the bicycle one of the most popular means of recreation and transportation around the world.

In 1839, Kirkpatrick Macmillan, a Scottish blacksmith, dramatically improved upon the original bicycle design. Macmillan's machine had tires with iron rims to keep them from getting worn down. He also used foot-operated cranks similar to pedals so his bicycle could be ridden at a quick pace. It didn't look much like a modern bicycle, though, because its back wheel was substantially larger than its front wheel. In 1861, the French Michaux brothers took the evolution of the bicycle a step further by inventing an improved crank mechanism.

Ten years later, James Starley, an English inventor, revolutionized bicycle design. He made the front wheel many times larger than the back wheel, put a gear on the pedals to make the bicycle more efficient, and lightened the wheels by using wire spokes. Although this bicycle was much lighter and less tiring to ride, it was still clumsy, extremely top-heavy, and ridden mostly for entertainment.

It wasn't until 1874 that the first truly modern bicycle appeared on the scene. Invented by another Englishman, H. J. Lawson, the "safety bicycle" would look familiar to today's cyclists. This bicycle had equal sized wheels, which made it less prone to toppling over. Lawson also attached a chain to the pedals to drive the rear wheel. With these improvements, the bicycle became extremely popular and useful for transportation. Today they are built, used, and enjoyed all over the world.

1. The main idea of this passage is best expressed in which sentence?
   a. Today, bicycles are so common that it's hard to believe they haven't always been around.
   b. It wasn't until 1874 that the first truly modern bicycle appeared on the scene.
   c. Since then, however, numerous innovations and improvements in design have made the bicycle one of the most popular means of recreation and transportation around the world.
   d. Today they are built, used, and enjoyed all over the world.

2. Which of the following would be the best title for this passage?
   a. Bicycles are Better
   b. A Ride through the History of Bicycles
   c. Cycle Your Way to Fitness
   d. The Popularity of Bicycles

3. Which sentence best expresses the main idea of the second paragraph?
   a. Macmillan was a great inventor.
   b. Macmillan's bike didn't look much like our modern bikes.
   c. Macmillan's bike could be ridden quickly.
   d. Macmillan made important changes in bicycle design.

4. An *innovation* is
   a. a new way of doing something
   b. a design
   c. an improvement
   d. a clever person

5. Macmillan added iron rims to the tires of his bicycle to
   a. add weight to the bicycle.
   b. make the tires last longer.
   c. make the ride less bumpy.
   d. make the ride less tiring.

6. The first person to use a gear system on bicycles was
   a. H. J. Lawson
   b. Kirkpatrick Macmillan
   c. The Michaux brothers
   d. James Starley

ANSWERS

PRACTICE 1

1. Who or what is this passage about?
   The U.S. Postal Service
2. How was mail delivered in the past?
   By horse or foot
3. How is mail delivered now?
   By trucks, trains, and planes
4. How long does first class mail take?
   Three days or less
5. How long does Priority Mail take?
   Three days or less
6. How long does Express Mail take?
   Overnight

PRACTICE 2

You should have underlined the last sentence: "Some lucky people have always know what they want to do with their lives." This sentence is a good topic sentence. It states the idea that holds the whole passage together. The first six sentences are specific examples of that idea.

Thus, they all support the main idea. This time, the topic sentence is at the end of the paragraph.

PRACTICE 3

1. **c.** The writer wasn't supposed to tell Nell about the surprise birthday party. Thus, a *blunder* is a mistake.

2. **a.** Honesty isn't a *problem*, so *b* can't be the answer. The passage says that the sales people have this *trait* in common. So *c* can't be correct either. The only words that makes sense in the sentence are *a, feature* or *aspect*.

3. **d.** You'd want to keep a copy for your records.

PRACTICE 4

Answers will vary. Here are some examples:

1. My job is very mundane. I do the same thing every day.

2. We left the picnic basket open. When we got back, it was teeming with ants.

PRACTICE 5

1. **F**

2. **O.** This is clearly something arguable. Many people enjoy watching the Olympics. But there are others who do not think it is fun. This is a matter of opinion.

3. **O.** Again, this is clearly something arguable.

4. **F**

5. **O.** here are many events at the Olympics. People have different opinions about which event they like best.

REVIEW PRACTICE

1. **c.** This is the only sentence general enough to encompass all of the ideas in the passage.

Each paragraph describes the innovations that led to the modern design of the bicycle, and this design has made it popular around the world.

2. **b.** The essay describes the history of the bicycle, from its invention in 1818 to its modern design.

3. **d.** Macmillan may have been a great inventor, but this paragraph only describes his innovations in bicycle design. The first sentence in this paragraph expresses this main idea in a clear topic sentence. The rest of the paragraph provides specific examples of the improvements he made in bicycle design.

4. **a.** An innovation is a new way of doing something. The first clue is in the third sentence, which describes the first bicycle—"it was made of wood and didn't even have pedals." Clearly, bicycles have changed dramatically. Other clues can be found in the following paragraphs, which describe the various changes made to bicycle design. Each bicycle designer came up with a new way of building a bicycle.

5. **b.** Since the question is asking for a specific fact about Macmillan's design, you should know to look in the second paragraph. Then you can find the sentence with the key words "iron rims"—the second sentence—to find the correct answer. This phrase is easy to find because it's been highlighted.

6. **d.** If you highlighted the various innovations, then all you have to do is scan the highlighted parts of the passage. Otherwise, you'd have to read through paragraphs 2, 3, and 4 to find the correct answer.

L·E·S·S·O·N 9

STRUCTURE

Understanding structure—how writers organize their ideas—will help you to understand what you read better. Writers decide how to arrange their sentences and ideas. They must decide which ideas go where, and they must choose how to move from one idea to another. Most writers organize their ideas in four patterns that help them effectively express their ideas:

- Time Order
- Order of Importance
- Compare and Contrast
- Cause and Effect

As you learn to recognize these four patterns in what you read, reading will become easier for you.

TIME ORDER

There are many ways to tell a story. Some stories start in the middle or at the end, but often, stories begin with what happened first. Then, they tell what happened next, and so on. They tell the story in the order in which the events occurred. This is called chronological order—chronology is the order in which things happen.

CHRONOLOGY AND TRANSITIONS

Much of what you read is ordered by chronology. Newspaper and magazine articles are usually arranged this way—so are meeting minutes and procedures. For example, look at the following paragraph. It is like something you might see in a company newsletter:

> Our employee awards dinner was a success. To begin, President Mike Smith announced the award for Perfect Attendance. Carlos Feliciano and Yelena Grishov were the winners. The second award was for Most Dedicated Employee. Jennifer Steele received this award. Then Mr. Smith made an announcement. He and his wife are expecting their first child. Afterwards, Vice President Jane Wu offered a toast. Next Mr. Smith gave the final award for Best New Idea. This award went to Karen Hunt. Finally, Mr. Smith ended the event with another surprise: He announced a 2% raise for all employees.

This paragraph describes what happened from start to finish. The writer used transitions to help you follow the order of events. Transitions tell readers that they are moving from one idea to another. They also show readers the relationship between ideas. For example, transitions may show that one event came before another. That's how they work in this passage. Notice the transitions *to begin, second, then, afterward, next,* and *finally* in the paragraph. They keep the events in chronological order. Thus, they are important tools to help readers follow ideas in the paragraph.

Without transitions, readers can't see the relationship between ideas. As a result, the paragraph sounds choppy, and readers don't know the order of events.

These transitions signal the chronology in a paragraph:

first	second
third, etc.	next
now	then
when	soon
before	after
during	while
meanwhile	in the meantime
immediately	suddenly
at last	eventually
finally	later
before long	shortly
as soon as	after a while

Transitions are one kind of clue that you should look for to help you figure out the order of events in a passage. These transitional words also help readers understand the relationship between ideas. Knowing the order of events is often important.

PRACTICE 1

Below is a list of transitions. Choose the ones that best fit into the paragraph. Write them in the blanks below. Check your answers at the end of this lesson.

> when
> as soon as
> yesterday
> then
> a moment later
> right away

_____I went to work early to get some extra filing done. _____I got there, the phone started ringing. _____my boss walked in. _____he asked me to type a letter. _____he asked me to set up a conference call. _____I looked at my watch, it was already 11 o'clock.

ORDER OF IMPORTANCE

Another way to present ideas is in order of importance. Once you understand this structure you'll see which ideas are most important in what you read.

Ideas can be organized by rank. Using this method, the first idea listed isn't the one that happened first, but rather it's the idea that's the most, or least, important. If writers start with the most important idea, then they would work down the line to the least important idea. Or they could do the reverse and start with the least important idea and build up to the idea that is most important.

MOST IMPORTANT
TO LEAST IMPORTANT

Sometimes passages begin with the most important idea. This often happens in newspaper articles. Readers want to know the most important facts right away: "Student protesters shut down the campus at UCLA today" or "City officials approved a tax cut." Writers choose this order so that readers will remember what they read first.

Here's a passage organized from the most important to the least important idea. Read it actively.

There are many ways to make tax time easier. The most important thing you can do is keep good records. Keep all of your pay stubs, receipts, and bank statements in a neat folder. When you're ready to prepare your tax form, all of your paperwork will be in one place. The second thing you can do is start early. Start filling out the forms as soon as they arrive in the mail. If you run into problems, you'll have plenty of time to sort them out. Finally, read the directions. This act can keep you from re-doing the form because you did it wrong the first time. It can also keep you from making mistakes.

The passage begins with a clear topic sentence. Then it offers three tax-time tips. The writer gives the most important tip first. "The most important thing you can do is keep good records."

What is the second most important thing you can do to make tax time easier? The writer started with the most important thing, meaning that the ideas are organized from most to least important. Thus, the second most important tip should come right after the first. The second best thing to do is "start early."

Finally, what's the third important tip the writer offers? The answer, of course is the last tip. You should "read the directions."

LEAST IMPORTANT
TO MOST IMPORTANT

Some writers organize ideas the opposite way. They don't start with the most important idea. Instead, they end with it. This order offers writers three advantages. First, readers are left with a strong conclusion. Second, this order makes use of the "snowball effect." Like a snowball rolling down a hill, the writer's ideas build and build. They get more and more important. Each idea builds on the ones that come before it. Third, starting with the least important idea creates suspense. Readers will be waiting to learn that final important idea.

You can often expect to see this structure in an argument. As the saying goes, "save the best for last." In an argument, the end is usually where "the best" has the most impact.

Writers usually choose their structure according to their purpose. And that structure affects how you understand what you read.

PRACTICE 2

Below is a list of reasons for reading more often. If you were to put these reasons in a paragraph, how would you organize them? First, rank the reasons in order of importance. Then rank them according to how you'd present them.

Five Reasons to Read More Often

- You will broaden your vocabulary.
- You will improve your reading comprehension.
- You will increase your reading speed.
- You will develop a better understanding of yourself and others.
- You will learn new information and ideas.

Order of Importance to You

1. _____
2. _____
3. _____
4. _____
5. _____

Order of Presentation

1. _____
2. _____
3. _____
4. _____
5. _____

In which order did you present your ideas? Most important to least important, or least important to most important? Either structure will work well with these ideas. Some writers want to hit their readers with what's most important at the beginning. Then they'll be sure to catch their readers' attention. Or they may want to save their best ideas for last. That way, readers build up to the most important idea.

Now that you've organized the ideas about reading that are listed above, put them into a paragraph. Add a topic sentence and transitions to the sentences listed.

_____
_____
_____
_____
_____
_____

COMPARISON AND CONTRAST

People spend a lot of time thinking about similarities and differences. When they want to explain similarities, they often compare the items. That will show how things are similar. Likewise, when they want to show how things are different, they contrast them to emphasize the differences between the items.

HOW COMPARING AND CONTRASTING WORKS

When people compare and contrast, they show how two things are similar or different. This helps others to judge the things that are being compared. For example, by comparing a cup of coffee to mud, you can give someone a good idea how the coffee looks and tastes.

Writers use comparison and contrast for the same reason. When you read, you can see how two or more things measure up side by side. What do they have in common? What sets them apart?

Read the following passage carefully to see how comparison and contrast work.

> Being a secretary is a lot like being a parent. A child is dependent upon her parent. Your boss is dependent on you. Children must ask for permission before they go out. Similarly, your boss will come to you for permission, too. You keep track of her schedule. "Can I have a meeting on Tuesday at 3:30?" your boss might ask. You'll also clean up after your boss. Just as a parent tucks toys away at the end of the day, you'll file papers, put things back into drawers, and tidy up the office. A parent protects his or her children from danger. Likewise, you'll find yourself protecting your boss from "dangers" like angry callers and clients. But there is one big difference. Children grow more independent each year. You boss will grow more dependent on you as the years go by.

Two things are being compared and contrasted here: a parent and a secretary. The writer lists four similarities between parents and secretaries:

1. Bosses depend upon secretaries like children depend upon their parents.
2. Bosses ask permission from their secretaries to do certain things just as children ask permission from their parents.
3. Secretaries clean up after their bosses like parents clean up after children.
4. Secretaries protect their bosses like parents protect their children.

Then the writer points out one difference between secretaries and parents. Children grow less and less dependent upon their parents. Meanwhile, bosses grow more and more dependent upon their secretaries.

Remember, writers always have a motive. So when you come across compare and contrast passages, ask yourself why the author is comparing those two items. What does the writer want you to get from the comparison? This comparison makes readers see secretaries in a new way. That's one of the values of this structure.

TRANSITIONS IN COMPARISON AND CONTRAST

Did you notice the transitions in the paragraph about secretaries and parents? Some transitions told you that the writer was comparing (showing a similarity). Others told you that the writer was contrasting (showing a difference). Go back and read the passage again. As you read it this time, underline the transitions.

There are several transitions that show comparison and contrast. You should have underlined *just like, similarly, also, much as, likewise, however,* and *on the other hand.* Below is a more complete list of transitional words and phrases.

Words that Help You Compare	
similarly	in the same way
likewise	in a like manner
like	just as, just like
also	much as, much like

Words that Help You Contrast	
but	on the contrary
however	on the other hand
yet	nevertheless
conversely	

PRACTICE 3

Compare and contrast the two items below. List three ways the two items are alike. Then list three was they are different. One similarity is listed to get you started. You can check your answers at the end of the lesson.

Item A: television
Item B: radio

Comparisons (similarities)

1. Both provide news and information
2. _____
3. _____

Contrasts (differences)

1. _____
2. _____
3. _____

CAUSE AND EFFECT

A passage about cause explains why something took place. On the other hand, a passage about effect explains what happened after something took place. Many reading passages explain cause or effect. You might read about the causes of World War I, or you could read about the effect of underwater nuclear testing. Because there are many cause and effect passages out there, it's important for you to recognize this structure.

TRANSITIONS FOR CAUSE AND EFFECT

Just as certain transitions tell readers whether two things are similar or different, or in what order events occur, other words tell readers whether things are causes or effects. Watch for these transitions as you read.

Words that Show Cause	
because (of)	created (by)
since	caused (by)

Words that Show Effect		
since	therefore	hence
so	consequently	as a result

OPINIONS ABOUT CAUSE AND EFFECT

Sometimes, writers offer their opinions about why something happened (cause). Or they might explain what they think will happen because of a certain event (effect). As a reader, you need to consider how reasonable those opinions are. Are the writers' ideas logical? Do writers' support the conclusions they offer?

As a reader you'll also have to decide which writer's opinions make more sense to you. Is the cause likely to have that result? Does the author's argument make sense?

PRACTICE 4

Below are two paragraphs. They consider how a no-smoking policy would affect an office. Read them carefully. Then answer the questions that follow. You can check your answers at the end of the lesson.

Paragraph A

A no-smoking policy would be disastrous. Over one-third of our employees smoke half a pack a day. If they can't smoke in the office, they'll have to leave the building. As a result, they'll have to take longer breaks. This will interrupt their work. They'll also have to take fewer breaks. And their breaks will be farther apart. This means longer stretches of time between cigarettes. Hence, many of these employees will be irritable. This irritability will surely affect their coworkers. Furthermore, long-time smokers may quit work, rather than put up with this strict policy.

Paragraph B

A no-smoking policy would be a great benefit to all of us. We'd be able to breathe smoke-free air. Furthermore, cigarette smell and smoke would no longer bother sensitive clients. In addition, smokers may find it easier to quit since they can't smoke as often during the day. Finally we will be able to cut the cost of healthcare coverage due to cigarette-related heath problems and save employees money.

1. What effects does Paragraph A say the no-smoking policy will have?
2. What effects does Paragraph B say the no-smoking policy will have?
3. What passage do you think sounds most reasonable? Why?

By now, you should have a good idea about the way writers organize their ideas. This new understanding should help you to figure out more easily what a passage means. Use what you have learned in this lesson to answer the following questions. Don't forget to use skills you learned in Lesson 8 also.

REVIEW PRACTICE

Read the following passage carefully and actively. Don't look up any unfamiliar words yet. First, try to figure out their meaning from context. Then answer the questions that follow.

There are many fatal mistakes businesses can make. The Right Stuff was a toy store. It sold stuffed animals. It closed after it made a promise it couldn't keep. The Right Stuff had only been open a few weeks. It ordered a large shipment of Wilbur, the popular stuffed dog. Then The Right Stuff ran an ad in the newspaper. The ad claimed that The Right Stuff had Wilbur in-stock and on-sale starting Sunday. But by Friday, the Wilburs hadn't arrived. The Right Stuff called the warehouse. They learned the toys were on back order. They wouldn't even ship until the next Thursday. What could The Right Stuff do? On Sunday, employees had to tell customers that there were no Wilbur dolls. They offered "I.O.U." coupons. But customers were mad. The sale was supposed to boost the store's business. Instead, it was a disaster. Two months later, The Right Stuff closed its doors for good.

1. Which two organizing strategies does this writer use?
   a. Time order
   b. Order of importance
   c. Compare and contrast
   d. Cause and effect

2. *Fatal* means
   a. Big
   b. Deadly
   c. Stupid
   d. Minor

3. What started the trouble for The Right Stuff?

4. What is the main idea of this paragraph?

Check your answers to see how you did. Could you see how each cause led to an effect? Could you see how each effect then caused another effect?

ANSWERS

PRACTICE 1—TIME ORDER

There are several ways to fill in the blanks. One option is below. Notice how much better the paragraph sounds with transitions.

> Yesterday I went to work early to get some extra filing done. As soon as I got there, the phone started ringing. A moment later my boss walked in. Right away he asked me to type a letter. Then he asked me to set up a conference call. When I looked at my watch, it was already 11 o'clock.

PRACTICE 2—ORDER OF IMPORTANCE

There are many ways to organize these ideas. Here's one example:

Order of Importance

1. You will develop a better understanding of yourself and others.
2. You will learn new information and ideas.
3. You will improve your reading comprehension.
4. You will broaden your vocabulary.
5. You will increase your reading speed.

Order of Presentation

1. You will develop a better understanding of yourself and others.
2. You will learn new information and ideas.
3. You will improve your reading comprehension.
4. You will broaden your vocabulary.
5. You will increase your reading speed.

The way your paragraph turns out depends on how you decided to order the ideas. The following are two sample paragraphs ordered from most to least important and from least to most important. The main idea is stated in the first sentence in each paragraph. The topic sentence is highlighted and the transitions are underlined.

Most to Least Important

There are many benefits to reading more often. First and foremost, reading more will give you a better understanding of yourself and others. You will also learn new information and ideas. Furthermore, you will improve your reading comprehension. You'll begin to understand more of what you read. In addition, you'll increase both your vocabulary and your reading speed.

Least to Most Important

There are many benefits to reading more often. First of all, by reading more, you will increase your reading speed. You'll be able to read more in less time. Second, you will broaden your vocabulary. Third, you will improve your reading comprehension. You'll understand more of what you read. Furthermore, you will learn new information and ideas. Most importantly, you will develop a better understanding of yourself and others.

PRACTICE 3—COMPARISON AND CONTRAST

Answers will vary. Here's one possibility

Comparisons (similarities)

1. Both provide news and information
2. Both need energy to run.
3. Both have commercials.

Contrasts (differences)

1. Radio is sound only. TV is sound and video.
2. Radio is mostly music and talk. TV has a lot more variety, including music, talk, drama, and comedy.

3. You can only get local radio stations. With cable you can get TV stations from all over the world.

PRACTICE 4

1. Paragraph A says that the no-smoking policy will have the following effects:

- Smokers will take longer breaks. This will interrupt their work.
- Smokers will have to take fewer breaks. This will make them irritable.
- Smokers' irritability will affect their coworkers.
- Long-time smokers may quit work.

2. Paragraph B says the no-smoking policy will have the following effects:

- Everyone will be able to breathe smoke-free air.
- Cigarette smell and smoke would no longer bother sensitive clients.
- Healthcare coverage would cost less.
- Employees will save money.

3. Answers will vary

REVIEW PRACTICE

1. The writer uses *a* and *d*—time order and cause and effect.

2. *Fatal* means *b* deadly. The main clue is that The Right Stuff closed down just two months after the incident.

3. The trouble was started by the ad. The first event in this chain reaction is ordering the Wilbur dogs. But that didn't cause the problem. The problem began with the ad. It said that the dogs were in stock.

4. The main idea of this paragraph is stated in the first sentence: "There are many fatal mistakes businesses can make." The rest of the passage gives a specific example of a mistake.

LANGUAGE AND STYLE

T he language and style a writer uses gives readers even more clues about the text. Sometimes, the main idea won't be stated directly, and you'll have to use these clues to understand what the author is trying to tell you. This lesson will help you understand how the language and style of a paragraph can help you understand what you are reading even better.

POINT OF VIEW

Point of view is the person or position through which you see things. People can look at an object from many different points of view. You can look at it from above, below, behind, beside, and so on. How you see the object depends on where you are looking from. In writing, the point of view is like a filter. It's the voice through which the writer shares his or her ideas. What readers learn from a text depends on who is telling it to them. Thus, point of view is an important decision for writers. Who will tell readers the writer's ideas? Who will narrate the story?

THREE POINTS OF VIEW

There are three points of view writers choose to use. They are the first person, second person, and third person points of view. A writer chooses the point of view depending upon the particular topic and purpose about which he is writing. The point of view helps a writer create a particular effect because each point of view works differently; each creates a different relationship between a reader and writer.

FIRST PERSON POINT OF VIEW

The first person point of view is a very personal point of view. The writer uses the pronouns *I* or *we* and thus shares his or her own feelings, experiences, and ideas with readers.

Example:

I knew I was going to be late, but there was no way to get in touch with my boss.

This point of view creates a closeness between the reader and writer. By using the pronouns, *I, my, mine, we, our,* or *us*, the writer or narrator shares his feelings or ideas with the reader. The relationship between reader and writer is personal and creates a feeling of confidentiality because the writer is talking directly to the reader.

SECOND PERSON POINT OF VIEW

In the second person point of view, writers use the pronoun *you*. The writer addresses the reader directly and makes the reader feel involved in the action.

Example:

You knew you were going to be late, but there was no way to get in touch with your boss.

The second person point of view singles you (as the reader) out as an individual and makes you feel a part of what the writer is writing about.

THIRD PERSON POINT OF VIEW

The third person point of view offers readers the voice of an "outsider." There is no direct reference to the writer (first person, "I/we") or the reader (second person, "you"). The writer uses the pronouns *he, she, it,* or *they*.

Example:

He knew he was going to be late. But there was no way to get in touch with his boss.

The third person point of view creates a distance between the reader and the writer (or narrator). With the third person point of view, there's no direct person-to-person contact (me to you). Rather, someone else is speaking to the reader.

PRACTICE 1

Change the point of view from third person to first person. Then check your answers at the end of the lesson.

1. The ad makes readers feel good about themselves.
2. The employees are upset about the hiring freeze.
3. People should keep the promises they make.

SUBJECTIVE VS. OBJECTIVE

The first person point of view is subjective (based on the thoughts, feelings, and experiences of the speaker or writer). However, ideas often carry more weight if they are objective (unaffected by the thoughts, feelings, and experiences of the speaker or writer). An objective person is outside of the action. He or she isn't personally involved; therefore, his or her ideas are likely to be more fair to everyone.

Example

Subjective: I don't like the bi-weekly pay period. Why should I have to wait two weeks to get paid?

Objective: The biweekly pay period is a problem. It's unfair to make employees wait two weeks to get paid.

Most people would say that the second passage makes a better argument. The subjective passage doesn't sound like a thoughtful argument. Instead, it sounds like a complaint. The first person, or subjective, point of view can create a wonderful closeness between writer and reader, but it's often less effective in an argument.

PRACTICE 1

Read the following sentences. Then decide which point of view is best for each situation. Check your answers at the end of this lesson.

1. You are a member of the city council. You are writing a letter to the editor of the local paper. Your purpose is to explain the township's new recycling program.
2. You are writing an editorial for the local paper. Your purpose is to convince readers to carpool.
3. You are writing a memo to your boss. Your purpose is to request a transfer.

WORD CHOICE

You already know that being observant is an important part of reading. Writers make a lot of decisions. They decide what to say and how to say it. They choose to use particular points of view and particular words for a reason. Some authors choose to clearly state their ideas, but sometimes, they *suggest* their ideas instead. They don't explicitly state their ideas; rather they leave clues

to tell the reader what the writer is saying. That's why it's important for readers to be observant.

Being observant means looking closely at what you read. By looking closely, you can see the writer's strategies, which will help you understand the text. You've already learned many of these strategies. For example, you know to look for the way writers arrange ideas. You also know to look for the point of view.

It's also helpful to look for:

- particular words phrases the writer uses
- how those words and phrases are arranged in sentences
- word or sentence patterns that are repeated
- important details about people, places, and things

THE IMPORTANCE OF WORD CHOICE

Even words that mean almost the same thing can make a different impression on a reader. For example, look at *slim* and *thin*. If you say your aunt is thin, that means one thing. If you say she is slim, that means something else. Slim has a different connotation (a word's suggested meaning) than thin. It's not about how the word is defined in a dictionary. It's about what the word makes you think or feel when you read it. Slim and thin have almost the same definition in the dictionary, but slim suggests more grace and class than thin. Slim is a very positive word. It suggests that your aunt is healthy. Thin, however, does not. Thin also suggests that your aunt is too skinny. Thin and slim then have different connotations. Therefore, the words authors choose to describe things can tell readers a lot.

Noticing word choice is especially important when the main idea of a reading passage isn't clear. For example, look at the following paragraph. It's a letter of recommendation. There's no topic sentence. Use your powers of observation to uncover the writer's message.

This letter is for my former office assistant, Jane Rosenberg. Jane usually completed her work on time. She proofread it carefully. She is an able typist. She is familiar with several word processing programs. She also knows some legal terms and procedures, which was helpful. Jane was always on-time. She always asked if she had a question.

Think about what message this letter sends to its reader:

A.   Jane Rosenberg is a great office assistant. Hire her right away!

B.   Jane Rosenberg is an average employee. She doesn't do outstanding work, but she's capable and reliable.

C.   Jane Rosenberg is a bad worker. Don't even think about hiring her.

Clearly, the writer does not think that Jane is an outstanding employee. Nor is she saying that Jane is a bad employee. The words she uses suggest that Jane is average. How can you come to this conclusion? By looking carefully at the words the writer has chosen, you can understand the writer's message.

OBSERVATION	CONCLUSION
The first sentence is neutral. The writer doesn't say, "I'm happy to recommend" or "my wonderful office assistant." The sentence is flat, without emotion.	The writer doesn't feel strongly about Jane. She doesn't want to suggest that Jane is a great employee. At the same time, she doesn't want to suggest that Jane would be a bad hire.
The writer uses "usually" in the second sentence.	Jane is good about meeting deadlines, but not great. She may not always get work done on-time.
The writer says that Jane proofreads her work carefully.	Jane makes sure she does quality work. She's not sloppy.
The writer calls Jane an "able" typist.	"Able" is a pretty neutral word; it suggests that Jane types well enough, but that she could do a lot better. She's probably not a very fast typist.
The writer say that Jane is "familiar with" several word processing programs.	Jane knows a little about the programs but isn't an expert. She can probably do a few basic things in each program, but she would have trouble doing complex projects.
The writer says that Jane knows "some legal terms and procedures."	Jane's knowledge of legal terms and procedures is limited. She knows a little, but not a lot. She's better than someone who knows nothing, but she's no expert.
The writer says Jane "was always on-time."	Jane is a reliable employee.
The writer says that Jane "always asked if she had a question	Jane won't assume things. If she's unsure, she'll ask because she wants to be sure she has it right.

PRACTICE 2

Now it's your turn. Below is another letter about Jane. Read the letter carefully. Then, fill in the chart. What do you see? What can you conclude from what you notice? Once you fill in the chart, answer the question that follows. When you are done, check your answers at the end of the lesson.

I am pleased to recommend my former office assistant, Jane Rosenberg. I could always count on Jane to get her work done on-time. I also knew she'd proofread it very carefully. In addition, she is an outstanding typist and has also mastered several word processing programs. Furthermore, she knows legal terms and procedures inside and out. That was a tremendous help. I could always count on Jane to be on-time, and I knew she's check with me if she had any questions.

OBSERVATION	CONCLUSION

Look at your observations and conclusions. What message is this writer sending?

A. Jane is a great office assistant. Hire her right away.

B. Jane is an average employee. She doesn't do outstanding work, but she's capable and reliable.

C. Jane is a bad worker. Don't even think about hiring her.

STYLE

Understanding style is very important to reading success. Writers use different structures to organize their ideas. They also use different styles to express those ideas. Being aware of style helps you see what writers are up to.

Style is also important for another reason. It's often what makes readers like or dislike certain writers or types of writing. You may not change your taste after this lesson, but you'll probably be able to appreciate and understand many different kinds of writers and styles. Style consists of three elements:

- sentence structure
- level of detail and description
- level of formality

SENTENCE STRUCTURE

Sentences can come in all kinds of shapes and sizes. They can be short and simple. Or they can be long and complex, with lots of ideas packed together. Writers can use mostly one kind of sentence or they can use a variety of sentence sizes, known as sentence structure. Some times sentences will all sound the same. Other times sentences will vary in word order and structure.

LEVEL OF DETAIL AND DESCRIPTION

The level of description and detail has a large effect on the reader. Some writers are quite descriptive. Others offer only a few details. Here are two things to consider:

1. How specific is the writer? Does he write "dog" (general) or "Labrador retriever" (specific)? Does she write "some" (general) or "three and a half pounds" (specific)?

2. How much description does the writer provide? Does he write "Mr. Zee is my manager" (non-descriptive)? Or does he offer some description: "Mr. Zee, my manager, is a tall man with piercing eyes and a mustache?" Or does he go even further: "Mr. Zee, my manager, is six-foot-ten with eyes that pierce like knives and a mustache like Charlie Chaplin" (very descriptive)?

Notice the increasing level of detail in the following examples. The first sentence is very general. The second sentence adds some detail. The third sentence gets even more specific.

1. Charles is a bank teller.
2. Charles is a bank teller at Pennview Savings.
3. Charles is a bank teller at Pennview Savings, the first bank in this city.

1. Let's meet after work on the corner.
2. Let's meet after work on the corner of 58th and Broadway.
3. Let's meet at 6:15 P.M. on the corner of 58th and Broadway.

PRACTICE 3

Change the style of the sentences below. Add specific description and detail. When you are done, check your answers at the end of the lesson.

1. He ate a huge breakfast this morning.
   Descriptive Version:

   _____
   _____
   _____
   _____

2. Please dress up for the party.
   Descriptive Version:

   _____
   _____
   _____
   _____

3. The new gym has lots of equipment.
   Descriptive Version:

   _____
   _____
   _____
   _____

LEVEL OF FORMALITY

Writers must decide how formal or informal they should be when they write. They decide the level of formality based on their audience and their purpose.

Writers can use slang, which is informal, proper language, or anything in between. They can address readers by their first names (casual) or by their title (formal). For example, the following sentences are two different levels of formality.

Your friend, Ted: Let's get together after work on Thursday.

Your boss, Mr. Brown: We invite you to join us for a social gathering at the close of business on Thursday.

Notice the drastic difference in style. The first sentence, directed at a friend is casual and informal. The second sentence, on the other hand, is very formal. Yet, both sentences send the same message; they just do it in different styles.

PRACTICE 4

Rank the following sentences below from 1–3 (1 is the most formal and 3 is the least formal). When you are done, check your answers at the end of the lesson.

1. _____Sales have improved.
   _____These figures show that sales have increased.
   _____Sales are up!

2. _____You're doing great work, O'Brien.
   _____Nice job, O'Brien.
   _____Your performance is above our expectations, O'Brien.

Thus, style is one way that helps writers express their ideas. Style consists of three elements: sentence structure, level of description and detail, and level of formality. Some writers use a very formal style while others are much casual. Style depends on the writer's audience and purpose.

REVIEW PRACTICE

Read the following passage carefully and answer the questions that follow. When you are done, check your answers at the end of the lesson.

Our company plans to merge with A+ systems, but the merger will have dire consequences for employees. First, the merger will force many of us to relocate. Second, many of us will be transferred to new departments. But most importantly, a merger means that hundreds of us will lose our jobs.

1. Which sentence states the main idea of this passage?
   a. The merger would be great for the company.
   b. The merger wouldn't change things too much.
   c. The merger would be bad for employees.

2. Which structure does this writer use to organize his ideas?
   a. time order
   b. cause and effect
   c. order of importance
   d. both b and c

3. Which point of view does the writer use in this passage?
   a. first person point of view
   b. second person point of view
   c. third person point of view

4. Based on the point of view, you can conclude that the writer is
   a. an employer
   b. an employee
   c. an outside consultant

5. The word *dire* means
   a. minimal
   b. expected
   c. disastrous

6. Which of the following best describes the style of this passage?
   a. very informal, casual
   b. descriptive, story-like
   c. formal, business like

You should be able to apply what you've learned to all that you read now. Now you know how authors write—you see how the words they use, the point of view from which they write, and the types of sentences they use to influence your understanding of a passage. You understand how authors use style to create meaning.

ANSWERS

PRACTICE 1

The changed pronouns are italicized below.

1. The ad makes *me* feel good about *myself*.
2. *I* am upset about the hiring freeze.
3. *I* should keep the promises *I* make.

PRACTICE 2

1.

OBSERVATION	CONCLUSION
The first sentence is very positive. The writer "is pleased" to recommend Jane.	The writer was very happy with Jane's work.
The writer says she could "always" count on Jane to get work done "on time."	Jane is a dependable worker. She meets deadlines.
The writer says she "knew" Jane would proofread "very carefully."	Jane is always careful about her work.
She calls Jane an "outstanding" typist.	Jane types quickly and correctly.
She says that Jane has "mastered" several word processing programs.	Jane knows those programs inside and out. She can create all kinds of documents on them.
She says that Jane knows legal terms and procedures "inside and out."	Jane really knows legal terms and procedures.
The writer "could always count on Jane" to be on-time.	Jane is never late.

2. **a.** From the high praise that Jane received, she will most likely be a great employee.

PRACTICE 3

Answers will vary. Here are some examples.

1. Celeste ate two scrambled eggs, three slices of bacon, and four pieces of buttered toast for breakfast this morning.
2. Please wear an evening gown or tuxedo for Thursday's holiday party.
3. The brand new gym has 7 Stairmasters, 20 stationary bikes, 25 treadmills, 3 sets of Nautilus equipment, 4 racquetball courts, and an Olympic-sized pool.

PRACTICE 4

1. 2, 3, 1
2. 2, 1, 3

REVIEW PRACTICE

1. **c.** The second sentence in the passage is the topic sentence. It states that the merger will be bad for employees. The other sentences in the paragraph support that idea.

2. **e.** The writer describes the effects of the merger (which is the cause) on the employees. She lists these effects in order of importance. She saves the most important effect for last.

3. **a.** The writer uses the first person pronouns our, us, and we.

4. **b.** The writer uses the first person point of view. Thus, you can conclude that she is an employee.

5. **c.** The consequences are all serious. They're all very negative. Thus, dire can't mean minimal. These effects may be expected (b). But the focus of the paragraph is the negative results.

6. **c.** The writer doesn't use any unneeded description or details. In fact, there aren't any details at all in this passage. It quickly gets to the point. There aren't any informal words or phrases. There's no suggestion that the writer and reader know each other well. There's a businesslike distance between reader and writer.

PUTTING IT ALL TOGETHER

So far you've studied how writers use structure and language to convey meaning to readers. Now it's time to put your new knowledge to work. In this lesson, you'll look at passages that don't have a clear main idea. You'll have to look carefully for clues. Then you can "read between the lines" to see what the author means.

FINDING AN IMPLIED MAIN IDEA

When the main idea is implied (hinted at) there is not necessarily any topic sentence, so finding the main idea can be a challenge. But, you already know about the importance of word choice and style. You know how to look carefully at the text to find clues that will help you figure out the main idea.

To find an implied main idea, you have to find an idea that is general enough to cover the whole paragraph. Choices that are too specific and do not include all of the ideas in the paragraph obviously cannot be the main idea of the paragraph. You must ask yourself which idea is supported by all of the sentences in the paragraph. You also need to look for words and phrases that point to this main idea.

PRACTICE PASSAGE 1

Read the paragraph below actively. Look for clues that suggest the main idea. Pay close attention to language. Notice how the writer describes Mr. Wilson. Then answer the questions that follow. Check your answers at the end of the lesson.

At 9:00 every morning, my boss, Mr. Wilson, invades the office. He marches straight to my desk and demands his reports. He spends the day looking over my shoulder and barking orders. And he blames every mistake—even if it's *his* fault—on me.

1. Which sentence states the main idea of the passage?
   a. It's a pleasure to work for Mr. Wilson.
   b. Mr. Wilson is a good manager.
   c. Mr. Wilson is bossy and unfair.
   d. Mr. Wilson is always on time.

2. How did you figure out the main idea? List some of the clues you found below.

_____

_____

_____

_____

_____

You saw a lot of clues in the practice passage above. They helped you determine the implied main idea. Perhaps you also noticed something else while studying the passage. What point of view does the writer use? She uses the first person. Her description is based on her personal experience and feelings. Thus, her view is subjective. An outsider might have a different opinion of Mr. Wilson.

INFERENCE

Inferences are conclusions that we draw based on the clues the writer has given us. When you draw inferences, you have to be something of a detective, looking for the clues (word choice, details, and so on) that suggest a certain conclusion, attitude, or point of view. You have to read between the lines in order to make a judgment about what an author was implying in the passage.

Questions that ask you about the meaning of vocabulary word in the passage and those that ask what the passage suggests or implies, are different from detail or main idea questions. Inference questions can be the most difficult to answer because they require you to draw meaning from the text when that meaning is implied rather than directly stated.

A good way to test whether you've drawn an acceptable inference is to ask yourself what evidence you have for the inference. If you can't find any, you probably have the wrong answer. You need to be sure that your inference is logical and based on something that is suggested or implied in the passage itself—not by an opinion you, or others, hold. Like a good detective, you need to base your conclusions on evidence—facts, details, and other information—not on random hunches or guesses.

PRACTICE PASSAGE 2

A good way to solidify what you've learned about reading comprehension questions is for you to write the questions. Write one question for each of the following four question types that you'll find on the Paragraph Comprehension portion of the ASVAB: fact or detail, main idea, inference, and vocabulary.

For or Against?—That Is the Question

Andy is the most unreasonable, pigheaded, subhuman life-form in the entire galaxy, and he makes me so angry I could scream! Of course, I love him like a brother. I sort of have to because he *is* my brother. More than that, he's my twin! That's right. Andy and Amy (that's me) have the same curly hair and dark eyes and equally stubborn temperaments. Yet, though we may look alike, on most issues we usually take diametrically opposite positions. If I say "day," you can count on Andy to say "night."

Just this week, the big buzz in school was all about the PTA's proposal to adopt a school dress code. Every student would be required to wear a uniform. Uniforms! Can you imagine? Oh, they won't be military-style uniforms, but the clothes would be uniform in color. The dress style would be sort of loose and liberal.

Boys would wear white or blue button-down shirts, a school tie, blue or gray pants, and a navy blue blazer or cardigan sweater. Girls would wear white or blue blouses or sweaters, blue or gray pants or skirts, along with a navy blue blazer or cardigan sweater. Socks or tights could be black, gray, blue, or white. The teachers are divided: some are in favor of the uniforms, others are opposed. The principal has asked the students to express their opinion by voting on the issue before making her decision. She will have the final word on the dress code.

I think a dress code is a good idea. The reason is simple. School is tough enough without worrying about looking cool every single day. The fact is, the less I have to decide first thing in the morning, the better. I can't tell you how many mornings I look into my closet and just stare, unable to decide what to wear. Of course, there are other mornings when my room looks like a cyclone had hit it, with bits and pieces of a dozen different possible outfits on the bed, on the floor, or dangling from the lamps. I also wouldn't mind not having to see guys wearing oversized jeans and shirts so huge they would fit a sumo wrestler. And, I certainly would welcome not seeing kids showing off designer-labeled clothes.

Andy is appalled at my opinion. He says he can't believe that I would be willing to give up my all-American teenage birthright by dressing like—well, like a typical teenager. Last night, he even dragged out Mom and Dad's high school photo albums. What a couple of peace-loving hippies they were!

"Bruce Springsteen never wore a school uniform. Bob Dylan wouldn't have been caught dead in a school uniform!" he declared. Andy was now on his soapbox. "When I am feeling political, I want to be able to wear clothes made of natural, undyed fibers, sewn or assembled in countries that do not pollute the environment or exploit child labor. If I have to wear a uniform, I won't feel like me!"

To which I replied, "So your personal heroes didn't wear school uniforms. Big deal! They went to high school about a million years ago! I feel sorry for you, brother dear. I had no idea that your ego is so fragile that it would be completely destroyed by gray or blue pants, a white or blue shirt, a tie, and a blazer."

That really made him angry. Then he said, "You're just mimicking what you hear that new music teacher saying because you have a crush on him!"

"That is so not true. He's just a very good teacher, that's all," I said, raising my voice in what mom would call "a very rude manner."

"You have always been a stupid goody-two-shoes, and you know it!" he snapped.

"Is that so? Anyone who doesn't agree with you is automatically stupid. And that's the stupidest thing of all!" I said.

Fortunately, the bell rang before we could do each other physical harm, and we went (thankfully) to our separate classes.

The vote for or against uniforms took place later that day. The results of the vote and the principal's decision will be announced next week. I wonder what it will be. I know how I voted, and I'm pretty sure I know how Andy voted.

How would you vote—for or against?

QUESTIONS

1. Detail Question:_____

_____

a. _____
b. _____
c. _____
d. _____

2. Main Idea Question:_____

_____

a. _____
b. _____
c. _____
d. _____

3. Inference Question:_____

_____

a. _____
b. _____
c. _____
d. _____

4. Vocabulary question:_____

_____

a. _____
b. _____
c. _____
d. _____

IMPLIED CAUSE AND EFFECT

Often writers have thoughts that they don't want to say directly. So they use suggestion to get their ideas across. They suggest cause in many ways. Some clues are action clues—what people said and did. Clues can also come in the form of details, word choice, and style. For example, look at the following passage.

Dennis was scared. His knees were weak. He looked down. The water was twenty feet below. He looked up again, quickly. He tried to think of something else. He tried to reassure himself. "It's only twenty feet!" he said aloud. But that only made it sound worse. Twenty feet! He felt dizzy and hot.

The writer could have said, "Dennis was scared. He was afraid of heights." Instead the writer *suggests* the cause. She *shows* you how Dennis feels. You see what he thinks and feels. Through these details, you can conclude that he's afraid of heights. The repetition of "20 feet" is another clue. So is the sentence structure. Notice that the sentences are short and choppy. In fact, they sound a little panicky. This helps show how Dennis felt.

PRACTICE PASSAGE 3

Below is an excerpt from a short story. Read the passage carefully. Then answer the questions that follow.

Anne tensed when she heard the front door open. She waited in the kitchen near the dirty dishes in the sink. She knew Stan would look there first. Taking a deep breath, she thought about what she would say to him. She waited.

A moment later, Stan stepped into the kitchen. She watched as he looked around the kitchen. His face hardened when he saw the dishes piled high in the sink. Pointing angrily at the dishes, he said coldly, "What are those filthy things still doing in the sink?"

"I haven't gotten to them yet," Anne replied. Her voice was equally cold.

"How many times have I told you? I want this house clean when I come home!"

"Oh every day. You tell me every single day. In fact, you tell me every day exactly what I should do and how I should do it. Do you think that you own me?"

"I do own this house, that's for sure. And I want my house clean!" Stan shouted.

"Then hire a maid," Anne said bitterly.

"What?"

"You heard me. Hire a maid—if you can find someone who can stand to work for you. You're never satisfied. And have you ever once said 'thank you?'"

Stan looked at Anne for a moment. His eyes were cold and hard. Then he turned and walked out of the room.

1. Why does Stan get mad?
   a. because Anne didn't get up to meet him at the door
   b. because he had a bad day at work
   c. because Anne didn't do the dishes
   d. because Anne is lazy

2. Why didn't Anne do the dishes?
   a. because she didn't have time to do them
   b. because she wanted to start a fight
   c. because she was too lazy
   d. because she wants Stan to hire a maid

3. Why is Anne mad at Stan?
   a. because he didn't say hello when he came home
   b. because they don't have a maid
   c. because he never helps around the house
   d. because he is too hard to please

Writers often suggest ideas, causes, and effects. You have to read between the lines to identify them. Look for clues in the action. What do people say and do? Look for more clues in details, word choice, and style. Use your sense of logic to answer questions and think about what the clues add up to.

REVIEW PRACTICE

Read the passage and answer the questions. Then check your answers at the end of the lesson.

Dealing with irritable patients is a great challenge for health care workers on every level. It is critical that you do not lose your patience when confronted by such a patient. When handling irate patients, be sure to remember that they are not angry with you; they are simply projecting their anger at something else onto you. Remember that if you respond to these patients as irritably as they act with you, you will only increase their hostility, making it much more difficult to give them proper treatment. The best thing to do is to remain calm and ignore any imprecations patients may hurl your way. Such patients may be irrational and may not realize what they're saying. Often, these patients will purposely try to anger you just to get some reaction out of you. If you react to this behavior with anger, they win by getting your attention, but you both lose because the patient is less likely to get proper care.

1. The word "irate" as it is used in the passage most nearly means:
   a. irregular, odd
   b. happy, cheerful
   c. ill-tempered, angry
   d. sloppy, lazy

2. The passage suggests that health care workers
   a. easily lose control of their emotions
   b. are better off not talking to their patients
   c. must be careful in dealing with irate patients because the patients may sue the hospital
   d. may provide inadequate treatment if they become angry at patients

3. An imprecation is most likely
   a. an object
   b. a curse
   c. a joke
   d. a medication

4. Which of the following best expresses the writer's views about irate patients?
   a. Some irate patients just want attention.
   b. Irate patients are always miserable.
   c. Irate patients should be made to wait for treatment.
   d. Managing irate patients is the key to a successful career.

By now, you should know what you need to pass the Paragraph Comprehension subtest. If you still want more practice, try these additional resources:

- Practice asking the four sample question types (see Practice 2 in this lesson) about passages you read for information or pleasure.
- Use your library. Many public libraries and school libraries have books with exercises to help your reading comprehension skills. It's a good idea to enlarge your base of information by reading related books and articles. Many libraries have computer systems that allow you to access information quickly and easily. Library personnel will show you how to use them and other resources.
- For more practice answering reading comprehension questions, you can also try another LearningExpress title *501 Reading Comprehension Questions* (LearningExpress, 1999).

ANSWERS

PRACTICE 1

1. **c.** The main idea is that Mr. Wilson is bossy and unfair.

2. There are lots of clues in the passage. First, the writer uses the word "invades." This word suggests that Mr. Wilson is trying to take over something that isn't his. It suggests that he isn't wanted. Second, Mr. Wilson spends the day "barking orders." He doesn't ask. He doesn't consider feelings. He just demands that things get done. Furthermore, the last sentence shows you that Wilson is unfair—*his* mistakes get blamed on someone else.

PRACTICE 2

Here is one question of each type based on the passage above. Your questions may be very different, but these will give you an idea of the kinds of questions that could be asked.

1. Detail question: Amy and Andy fight because
   a. neither one is able to convince the other to change his or her point of view.
   b. they're both stubborn.
   c. they always take the opposite view on issues.
   d. they don't like each other very much.

2. Main idea question: Which of the following is the best statement of Andy's position on the issue presented in the story?
   a. School clothing should reflect parents' values.
   b. Wearing school uniforms means one less decision every morning.

c. How one dresses should be an expression of one's personality.
d. Teenagers should never follow the latest fads in dress.

3. Inference question: Amy's position on school uniforms is most likely based on
   a. logical conclusions drawn on her own observation and personal experience.
   b. an emotional response to what she has been told by people in authority.
   c. her preference for designer-labeled clothes.
   d. not liking anything her brother likes.

4. Vocabulary question: Read the following sentences from the story:

   Andy is <u>appalled at</u> my opinion. He says he can't believe that I would be willing to give up my all-American teenage birthright by dressing like—well, like a typical teenager.

   As it is used in these sentences, what does *appalled at* mean?
   a. angry
   b. in denial
   c. supportive of
   d. horrified by

PRACTICE 3

1. **c.** He doesn't get mad until he sees the dishes in the sink. You can tell he expects the kitchen to be clean when he comes home. When he walks in, he looks around the kitchen. It's as if he's inspecting it. Then he sees the dishes and his face hardens. He asks why they're in the sink. Furthermore, he tells Anne that he wants the house clean when he comes home.

2. b. You can tell Anne wants to start a fight from the first paragraph. She purposely waits in the kitchen near the dirty dishes. She knows Stan is going to be mad about the dishes when he sees them. As she waits, she thinks about what she's going to say to him.

3. d. Anne's response to Stan tells you why she's mad. She's tired of him telling her what to do "every blessed day." She feels like he owns her. She's also frustrated because he's "never satisfied." And she's mad because he has never "once said 'thank you.'"

REVIEW PRACTICE

1. c. This is a vocabulary question. Irate means ill-tempered, angry. It should be clear that **b**, happy, cheerful, is not the answer; dealing with happy patients is normally not "a great challenge." Patients that are **a**, irregular, odd, or **d**, sloppy, lazy, may be a challenge in their own way, but they aren't likely to rouse health care workers to anger. In addition, the passage explains that irate patients are not "angry at you," and irate is used as a synonym for irritable, which describes the patients under discussion in the very first sentence.

2. d. This is an inference question, as the phrase "the passage suggests" might have told you. The idea that angry health care workers might give inadequate treatment is implied by the passage as a whole, which seems to be an attempt to prevent angry reactions to irate patients. Furthermore, the last sentence in particular makes this inference possible: "If you react

to this behavior with anger . . . you both lose because the patient is less likely to get proper care." Answer **c** is not correct, because while it may be true that some irate patients have sued the hospital in the past, there is no mention of suits anywhere in this passage. Likewise, answer **b** is incorrect; the passage does suggest ignoring patients' insults, but nowhere does it recommend not talking to patients—it simply recommends not talking angrily. And while it may be true that some health care workers may lose control of their emotions, the passage does not provide any facts or details to support answer **a**, that they "easily lose control." Watch out for key words like *easily* that may distort the intent of the passage.

3. b. If you didn't know what an imprecation is, the context should reveal that it's something you can ignore, so neither **a**, an object, nor **d**, a medication, is a likely answer. Furthermore, **c** is not likely either, since an irate patient is not likely to be making jokes.

4. a. The writer seems to believe that some irate patients just want attention, as is suggested when the writer says, "Often these patients will purposely try to anger you just to get some reaction our of you. If you react to this behavior with anger, they win by getting your attention." It should be clear that **a** cannot be the answer because it includes an absolute: "Irate patients are always miserable." Perhaps some of the patients are often miserable, but an absolute like *always* is almost always wrong. Besides, this passage refers to patients who may be irate in the hospital, but we have no indication of what there patients are like at other times, and miserable and irate are not exactly the same thing either. Answer **c** is also incorrect because the purpose of the passage is to ensure that patients receive "proper treatment" and that irate patients are not discriminated against because of their behavior. Thus, "irate patients should be made to wait for treatment" is not a logical answer. Finally, **d** cannot be correct because although it may be true, there is no discussion of career advancement in the passage.

S·E·C·T·I·O·N 4

VOCABULARY FOR THE WORD KNOWLEDGE SUBTEST

Good communication skills—including vocabulary and spelling—are essential to everything you do. A good vocabulary increases your ability to understand reading material and to express yourself both in speaking and in writing. Without a broad vocabulary, your ability to learn is limited. The good news is that vocabulary skills can be developed with practice. The Word Knowledge portion of the ASVAB is basically a vocabulary test.

Combined with the Paragraph Comprehension score, Word Knowledge helps make up your Verbal Equivalent score—it's one of the all-important subtests that determine whether you'll be allowed to enlist. Your ability to understand your training materials depends in part on your reading comprehension and vocabulary skills

There are two different kinds of questions on the Word Knowledge subtest:

- Synonyms: Identifying words that mean the same as the given words
- Context: Determining the meaning of a word or phrase by noting how it is used in a sentence or paragraph.

You already have had some practice identifying the meanings of words by examining their context in Section 3: Reading Comprehension for the Paragraph Comprehension Subtest. You will get some more practice in this section, and you will also learn about synonyms and word parts, including word roots, prefixes, and suffixes. These lessons will help you improve and develop your vocabulary skills, teaching you how to break down words into parts you recognize so that you can decipher their meanings. Remember, you are not penalized for guessing on the ASVAB, so these methods will help you improve your guessing power when you encounter unknown words on the Word Knowledge subtest.

Each of us has three vocabularies in each language that we speak:

- A **speaking** vocabulary: the words and expressions we use every day to communicate.
- A **listening** vocabulary: words and expressions we have heard but may have never used.
- A **reading** vocabulary: words and expressions we have encountered in print but have neither heard not used.

One of the best ways to increase your vocabulary is to make a conscious effort to move words from your listening or reading vocabularies to your speaking vocabulary—the words that you not only understand, but also use.

There are three ways we learn vocabulary:

- from the **sound** of words
- from the **structure** of words
- from the **context**, how the word is used

Learning words then is a three-step process.

1. Ask yourself, "Does this word **sound** like anything I've ever heard?"

If not, ask
2. "Does any part of the word **look** familiar?"

If not, then ask
3. "How is this word **used** in the sentence I read or heard?"

Try asking yourself this sequence of questions with each unfamiliar word you encounter in this section. As you learn more about how vocabulary works, you'll find that you already know some of the words, and you can use your new knowledge to figure out the others.

L·E·S·S·O·N
WORD PARTS
12

The value of learning word parts is that they act as a kind of access key that gives you clues about other words that are in the same "family" as the word you know. Roots, prefixes, and suffixes are word elements that share characteristics, much as human beings in families share names and other personal attributes.

English words share so many traits because they descend from a long line of intermingled languages from the Indo-European family of languages. Many English words come from the Greek and Latin languages, which gave us much of our culture through the ages. Again, the point of learning to recognize word parts is that they give you access to whole groups of words when you know a few prolific "families."

The best way to improve your vocabulary is to learn word parts. Using word parts to increase vocabulary works in two ways:

1. You may already know a given root, prefix, or suffix that can guide you in determining the meaning of an unfamiliar word. For example, you may know that the root *hydro* suggests water. Therefore, if you came across the word *hydrotherapy*, you would figure it is a treatment that uses water.

2. If you don't know the part by itself, you may recognize it from a word you know. By association, then, you link the known meaning to that of an unfamiliar word. For example, you know that a fire hydrant stores water. Therefore, you associate the root *hydro* to water and come up with the meaning of *hydrotherapy*.

ROOTS

Roots are the pieces of words that carry direct meaning. Generally roots of English words are derived from ancient Greek and Latin words. Because so many English words have their source in certain recurring root words, knowing some of the most commonly used roots gives you access to many words at once. When you combine your knowledge of roots with your knowledge of prefixes and suffixes, the small parts of words that go at the beginning or end of words to change their meanings, you have the tools for figuring out the meanings of many words from their structure.

DEFINITIONS AND ROOTS

The value of learning roots is that they act as a kind of access key that gives you clues about other words that share the roots or "family lineage" of the word you know.

Below are the definitions and roots of some words, along with some other words that share their roots.

agoraphobic (phobe = fear): fear of open spaces
phobia, claustrophobia, xenophobia

antagonize (agon = struggle, contest): to struggle against
protagonist, agony, agonize

assimilate (simul = copy): to fit in
similar, simile, facsimile, simulate

attribute (trib = to give): a special quality
tributary, contribution, tribunal

audible (aud = hear): able to be heard
audition, audit, auditorium

belligerent (bell = war): warlike
bellicose, antebellum

benevolent (ben = good): kind
benefactor, beneficiary, benign, benediction

biodegradable (bio = life): able to be broken down by living things
bionic, biology, antibiotic

chronic (chron = time): occurring over time
chronological, chronometer, chronicle

conspicuous (spic, spec = see): highly visible
spectacle, spectator, inspection, introspection

contradiction (contra = against, dict = say): the act or state of disagreeing
dictate, dictionary, interdict, dictation

credence (cred = believe): belief, believability
creed, credulous, credit, incredible

demographic (demo = people): having to do with the measurement of populations
democracy, demagogue

evident (vid = see): obvious
video, evidence, visible, provident

fidelity (fid = faith): faithfulness
Fido, fiduciary, infidel, infidelity

fluctuate (flux, flu = to flow): to rise and fall
fluid, fluidity, superfluous, influx

gregarious (greg = crowd, herd): sociable
egregious

impediment (ped, pod = foot; ped also means child): a barrier or hindrance
pedestal, pedestrian, pediment

incisive (cis, cid = to cut): penetrating, clear cut
incision, precise, scissors, homicide, suicide

incognito (cog, gno = to know): unrecognizable
diagnosis, recognize, cognition, cognitive

inducement (duc = to lead): leading to an action
induction, reduction, introduction, reduce

inference (fer = bear or carry): guess or surmise
transfer, refer, reference, interfere

interrogate (rog = to ask): to question
surrogate, derogatory, arrogant

loquacious (loq = speak): talkative
   eloquent, soliloquy
mediocre (med = middle): of medium quality,
   neither good nor bad
   media, median, intermediate, mediator
nominal (nom, nym = name): in name only
   nominate, nomenclature, synonym, anony-
   mous
pathos (path = feeling): feeling of sympathy or
   pity
   pathetic, empathy, sympathy, pathology, apathy
philanthropy (phil = love): giving generously to
   worthy causes
   philosophy, Philadelphia, bibliophile
precedent (ced = go): a prior ruling or
   experience
   intercede, procedure, succeed
protracted (tract = draw, pull): dragged out
   tractor, distracted, attraction, subtracted
recapitulate (cap = head): to review in detail
   capital, caption, captain, decapitate
rejected (ject = to throw or send): sent back
   subject, dejected, interjected, projectile
remittance (mit, mis = to send): to pay or send
   back
   submit, commission, permission, intermission
sophisticated (soph = wisdom): having style or
   knowledge
   sophomore, sophistry, philosopher
tangential (tang, tac, tig = touch): touching
   slightly
   tangent, tactical, tactile, contiguous
tenacious (ten = hold): unwilling to let go,
   stubborn
   tenacity, contain, tenable

urbane (urb = city): polished, sophisticated
   urban, suburban, urbanite
verify (ver = truth): to establish as truth
   verity, veritable, veracious, aver
vivacious (viv = life): lively in manner
   vivid, vital, vivisection

PRACTICE 1

Fill in the blanks with words from the previous list.
Check your answers at the end of the lesson.

1. His remarks were _____ and cut right
   to the heart of the subject.
2. It doesn't pay to _____ the opinions of
   those who are in authority.
3. His _____ arose from his deep desire
   to help those less fortunate than himself.
4. The store demanded the _____ of the
   payment required to clear the debt.
5. One of her best _____ is her clear-eyed
   wisdom.
6. Over the years, people from many countries
   have come to _____ into American life.
7. Public works projects in the 1930s set a
   _____ for social legislation for the next
   60 years.
8. After the game, the commentators continued to
   _____ the key plays for those who had
   been unable to watch it.
9. She believed that her working life was merely
   _____ to the "real life" she enjoyed with
   her family.
10. Scientists need to develop a _____ trash
    bag that would lessen the problem of waste
    removal to landfill areas.

PRACTICE 2

Answer the following with words from the previous list. Check your answers at the end of the lesson.

1. Which word stems from a root that means good? _____

2. Which word stems from a root than can mean foot or child? _____

3. Which word stems from a root that means to cut or kill? _____

4. Which word stems from a root that means to bear or carry? _____

5. Which word stems from a root than means a fear? _____

6. Which word stems from a root that means love?

7. Which word stems from a root that suggests touching? _____

8. Which word stems from a root that means belief? _____

9. Which word stems from a root that suggests speaking? _____

10. Which word stems from a root that suggests life? _____

PREFIXES

Prefixes are word parts at the beginning of a word that change or add to the meaning of the root word in some way. They are often seen in different forms and may fundamentally change the meaning of a root word—making it an opposite, for example. Or a prefix may only remotely suggest meaning. The point of working with prefixes is not to memorize a batch of disconnected word parts but to become familiar with the most common examples. Then you may be able to figure out how a word's meaning may have been affected by a prefix.

For example, the Latin root *vert* means to turn. Look at what happens when you add different prefixes in front of that root:

- con (with or together) + vert = convert (transform—think turn together)
  She wanted to **convert** the old barn into a studio.
- di (two) + vert = divert (turn aside)
  He wanted to **divert** attention from his shady past.
- ex (out of, away from) + vert = extrovert (an outgoing, out-turning, individual)
  He was an **extrovert** who was the life of every party.
- in (opposite) + vert = invert (turn over)
  He **inverted** the saucer over the cup.
- intro (inside) + vert = introvert (an inwardly directed person)
  She was an **introvert** who generally shied away from company.
- re (back or again) + vert = revert (turn back)
  He **reverted** to his old ways when he got out of prison.

DEFINITIONS AND PREFIXES

Below are some words with their prefixes and meanings, as well as other words that use the prefix.

antecedents (ante = before): something that comes before, especially ancestors
   antenatal, antebellum, anteroom
antipathy (anti = against) hatred, feelings against
   antiwar, antibiotic, antidote
circumvent (circum, circ = around): to get around
   circumscribe, circulate, circumference

consensus (con = with, together): agreement on a course of action
congress, convivial, congregate

controversy (contr = against): public dispute
contraceptive, contrast, contrary

decimate (dec = ten): to destroy or kill a large portion of something
decimal, decibel

demote (de = down, away from): to lower in grade or position
decline, denigrate, deflate

disinterested (dis = not, opposite of): not having selfish interest in (not the same as uninterested)
disappointed, disabled, disqualified

euphemism (eu = good, well): a more pleasant term for something distasteful
euthanasia, euphonious, eugenic

exorbitant (ex = out of, away from): excessive (literally, out of orbit)
exhume, extort, exhale, export

illegible (il = not, opposite): not readable
illegal, illegitimate, illicit

intermittent (inter = between): occurring from time to time, occasional
intermediate, interlude, intermission, interview

malevolent (mal = bad): cruel, evil
malady, malefactor, malice, malignant

precursor (pre = before): a form that precedes a current model
premeditate, premature, prevent, preview

prognosis (pro = before): opinion about the future state of something
provide, professional, produce

retrospect (retro = back, again): hindsight
retroactive, retrograde, retrorocket

subordinate (sub = under): lower in rank
subterranean, substrate, subscription

synthesis (syn, sym = with or together): the combination of many things into one
synthetic, symphony, symbiotic

transcend (trans = across): to go beyond
transfer, transportation, transatlantic

trivial (tri = three): unimportant
tripod, triangle, triennial

Note that some words translate very neatly into their components:

- Antipathy means literally feelings against (anti = against, path = feelings).
- Retrospect means literally looking back (retro = back, spect = to look or see).

But beware, in some cases, the connection between the meaning of the prefix and the meaning of the word is much less obvious. For instance, the word trivial comes from the place where, in ancient times, the three main caravan routes met and people exchanged gossip and bits of information. Today we use trivial to refer to small items of information that are relatively unimportant.

PRACTICE 3

Complete each of the sentences below with a word from the previous list. Check your answers at the end of the lesson.

1. The manager threatened to _____ the clerk if he came late one more time.
2. The union leaders finally reached a(n) _____ over the salary package.

3. The Civil War _____ both the land and the population of the South.

4. The jumbo jets were the _____ of today's SSTs.

5. The choice had to be made by a(n) _____ person who would not benefit from the outcome.

6. Using too many _____ to avoid distasteful subjects weakens our ability to express ourselves clearly.

7. The boy always found a way to _____ authority and get his own way.

8. She likes to meditate on the words of the great philosophers in order to _____ her mundane concerns.

9. Many people focus on the _____ things in life and ignore the more important matters.

10. _____ is unavoidable when two political parties try to come to an agreement.

PRACTICE 4

Mark the following statements as true or false according to the meaning of the underlined word. Check your answers at the end of the lesson.

1. Most people would want to pay an <u>exorbitant</u> sum for a theater ticket.

2. An <u>intermittent</u> action doesn't just happen once.

3. A <u>retrospective</u> exhibition shows only recent works by an artist.

4. A <u>disinterested</u> person is bored with her work.

5. A <u>consensus</u> opinion represents the group that makes the decision.

6. A <u>malevolent</u> character in a movie is usually the hero.

7. One's children are one's <u>antecedents</u>.

8. Only <u>trivial</u> matters are referred to the CEO of the company.

9. If you have <u>antipathy</u> toward someone, you have little or no feeling at all.

10. We use <u>euphemisms</u> when we want to soften the meaning of what we say.

SUFFIXES

You may remember from elementary school English classes that words are divided into something called parts of speech—primarily nouns (people, places, and things), verbs (action or existence words), and adjectives and adverbs (words which describe other words). Suffixes often change the part of speech of a word.

Thus, adding a suffix often changes the function of the word in a sentence without fundamentally changing the word's meaning. You can think of a suffix as the "outfit," or "uniform," a word wears for a particular job in the sentence, just as you may wear different outfits for different activities: a suit or uniform for work, jeans for household chores, and a track suit for jogging.

For example, take the word *devote*, meaning to dedicate time to the care of someone or something. Suffixes change the way the word works in a sentence.

- As a **verb**, it appears as it is:
  I will *devote* my time to my family.
- As a **noun**, it "wears" the **-tion** suffix and becomes devotion:
  His *devotion* to his family was well known.
- As an **adjective** modifying a noun, it wears the **-ed** suffix:
  He is a *devoted* family man.

- As an **adverb** modifying a verb, it wears the **ly** suffix:
  He served his family *devotedly* for many years.

The table that follows shows commonly used suffixes. They are divided into the parts of speech or the "jobs" they suggest for the words. Other words that contain those suffixes are listed. In the last column, you can add at least one other word you already know that uses the same suffix.

Suffix	Meaning	Examples	Your Example
Noun Endings			
-tion	Act or state of	retraction, contraction	
-ment	Quality of	deportment, impediment	
-ist	One who	feminist, philanthropist	
-ism	State or doctrine of	barbarism, materialism	
-ity	State of being	futility, civility	
-ology	Study of	biology, psychology	
-escence	State of	adolescence, convalescence	
-y, -ry	State of	mimicry, trickery	
Adjective Endings			
-able	Capable of	perishable, flammable	
-ic	Causing, making	nostalgic, fatalistic	
-ian	One who is or does	tactician, patrician	
-ile	Pertaining to	senile, servile	
-ious	Having the quality of	religious, glorious	
-ive	Having the nature of	sensitive, divisive	
-less	Without	guileless, reckless	
Verb Endings			
-ize	To bring about	colonize, plagarize	
-ate	To make	decimate, tolerate	
-ify	To make	beautify, electrify	

DEFINITIONS AND SUFFIXES

Below are some words with their suffixes and meanings. The words contain highlighted suffixes that identify the word as working at a particular job in the sentence. As you look at the words, think about words you already know that contain the same suffix.

agrar**ian**: having to do with agriculture or farming

> The farmer loved his agrarian life.

bigo**try**: narrow-minded intolerance

> We must guard against bigotry wherever it exists.

consumm**ate**: to make complete

> The deal was consummated after long negotiations.

cop**ious**: plentiful

> He shed copious tears over the tragic bombing.

cryp**tic**: mysterious, hidden

> She made a cryptic comment that was unclear to everyone.

defer**ment**: delay

> He wanted a deferment on paying his student loans.

etym**ology**: study of word origins

> The scholar was an authority on the etymology of words.

furt**ive**: underhanded and sly

> He had a furtive manner.

laud**able**: praiseworthy

> He had laudable intentions to do good in his community.

muta**tion**: a change in form

> The scientist found a significant mutation in the gene.

obsol**escence**: the state of being outdated

> The new designs were already headed for obsolescence.

par**ity**: equality

> He wanted parity with the other employees.

pragmat**ism**: faith in the practical approach

> His pragmatism helped him run a successful business.

protagon**ist**: one who is the central figure in a drama

> The protagonist was played by a great actor.

provoca**tive**: inciting to action

> The actions of a few demonstrators were provocative.

puer**ile**: childish

> The father's actions were puerile; his five-year-old was more mature.

rect**ify**: to correct

> He wanted to rectify the misunderstanding.

relent**less**: unstoppable

> He was relentless in his search for knowledge.

sati**rize**: to use humor to expose folly in institutions or people

> Comedians like to satirize politicians.

vener**ate**: to respect or worship

> He venerated his parents and protected their interests.

PRACTICE 5

Mark the following statements as true or false according to the meanings of the underlined words. Check your answers at the end of the lesson.

1. _____ A <u>deferment</u> allows immediate action.

2. _____The <u>protagonist</u> is usually the most important person in a play.

3. _____Most people think that wage <u>parity</u> is a good idea, at least in theory.

4. _____ <u>Obsolescence</u> adds value to merchandise.

5. _____ <u>Etymology</u> is the study of insect life.

6. _____A <u>mutation</u> can be a change of form.

7. _____A <u>relentless</u> search is over quickly.

8. _____ <u>Provocative</u> comments are usually comical.

9. _____A <u>furtive</u> glance is sly and secretive.

10. _____ <u>Agrarian</u> life is found in the city.

Practice 6

Complete the following sentences. Check your answers at the end of the lesson.

1. If you venerate something, you _____

_____ .

2. If you request a deferment, you want _____

_____ .

3. If you want to rectify a situation, you must

_____ .

4. If you are a relentless person, you _____

_____ .

5. If your motives are laudable, they are _____

_____ .

6. If you satirize something, you _____

_____ .

7. If you behave in a puerile manner, you are ___

_____ .

8. If you behave in a furtive way, you are being

_____ .

9. If you want parity at work, you wan _____

_____ .

10. If you consummate arrangements for a trip,

you _____

_____ .

By now you should be familiar with many word parts, from roots, to prefixes, to suffixes. You have not only learned new words, but you have also learned how to identify unfamiliar words by identifying parts of the word that you already know.

ANSWERS

PRACTICE 1
1. incisive
2. contradict
3. philanthropy
4. remittance
5. attributes
6. assimilate
7. precedent
8. recapitulate
9. tangential
10. biodegradable

PRACTICE 2
1. benevolent
2. impediment
3. incisive
4. inference
5. agoraphobia
6. philanthropy
7. tangential
8. credence
9. contradict
10. biodegradable

PRACTICE 3
1. demote
2. consensus
3. decimated
4. precursors
5. disinterested
6. euphemisms
7. circumvent
8. transcend
9. trivial
10. controversy

PRACTICE 4
1. false
2. true
3. false
4. false
5. true
6. false
7. false
8. false
9. false
10. true

PRACTICE 5
1. false
2. true
3. true
4. false
5. false
6. true
7. false
8. false
9. true
10. false

PRACTICE 6
1. respect it
2. a postponement
3. correct it
4. don't give up
5. praiseworthy
6. make fun of it
7. childish
8. sly and sneaky
9. equal treatment
10. finalize them

WORDS IN CONTEXT

Since you have already learned about context in Lesson 8 of the Reading Comprehension section, this lesson is mostly practice questions to get you ready for the ASVAB.

Context is the surrounding text in which a word is used. Most people use context to help them determine the meaning of an unknown word. A vocabulary question that gives you a sentence around the vocabulary word is usually easier to answer than one with little or no context. The surrounding text can help you as you look for synonyms for specified words in the sentences.

The best way to take meaning from context is to look for key words in sentences or paragraphs that convey the meaning of the text. If nothing else, the context will give you a means to eliminate wrong answer choices that clearly don't fit. The process of elimination will often leave you with the correct answer.

PRACTICE 1

Choose the word that best fills the blank in the following sentences. Check your answers at the end of the lesson.

1. The main _____ Jim had was too many parking tickets.
   a. disaster
   b. search
   c. request
   d. problem

2. While trying to _____ his pet iguana from a tree, Travis Stevens fell and broke his ankle.
   a. examine
   b. transfer
   c. rescue
   d. pardon

3. When I bought my fancy car, I didn't stop to _____ how I'd pay for it.
   a. consider
   b. promote
   c. require
   d. adjust

4. We knew nothing about Betty, because she was so _____.
   a. expressive
   b. secretive
   c. emotional
   d. artistic

5. We were tired when we reached the _____, but the spectacular view of the valley below was worth the hike.
   a. circumference
   b. summit
   c. fulcrum
   d. nadir

6. The _____ of not turning in your homework is after-school detention.
   a. reward
   b. denial
   c. consequence
   d. cause

7. His suit had a(n) _____ odor, as if it had been closed up for a long time in an old trunk.
   a. aged
   b. dried-up
   c. musty
   d. decrepit

8. Every day he had to deal with crowds of noisy, demanding people, so he longed most of all for _____.
   a. solitude
   b. association
   c. loneliness
   d. irrelevancy

9. Julia was blamed for the town's bad fortune, and so she was _____ by everyone.
   a. regarded
   b. shunned
   c. neglected
   d. forewarned

10. When Bobby Wilcox let a frog loose in class, Ms. Willy became so _____ that she threw an eraser.
    a. animated
    b. incautious
    c. irate
    d. irradiated

11. The star's _____ remarks about other actors with whom he had worked made the whole company careful about what they said in front of him.
   a. spiteful
   b. changeable
   c. approving
   d. prudent

12. The teacher put the crayons on the bottom shelf to make them _____ to the young children.
   a. accessible
   b. receptive
   c. eloquent
   d. ambiguous

13. My computer was state-of-the-art when I bought it five years ago, but now it is _____.
   a. current
   b. dedicated
   c. unnecessary
   d. outmoded

14. Lola had been traveling for weeks; she was on a _____ to find the perfect cup of coffee.
   a. surge
   b. quest
   c. discovery
   d. cadence

15. Roland developed an _____ plan to earn extra money to buy the computer he had always wanted.
   a. elitist
   b. irrational
   c. aloof
   d. ingenious

16. George is _____ because he is the only one on staff who knows how to use this computer program.
   a. frustrated
   b. prudent
   c. indispensable
   d. creative

17. Harrison needs help; he's a _____ gambler.
   a. cheerful
   b. phantom
   c. bucolic
   d. chronic

18. I do not like your negative attitude, and it has _____ affected our working relationship.
   a. favorably
   b. adversely
   c. shamelessly
   d. candidly

PRACTICE 2

Choose the word that best fills the blank in the following sentences. Check your answers at the end of the lesson.

1. It's easy to take care of my cousin's dog Sparky; he's a _____ and obedient pet.
   a. delectable
   b. commonplace
   c. meddlesome
   d. docile

2. I had no trouble finding your house; your directions were _____.
a. priceless
b. arduous
c. explicit
d. embodied

3. Though the principal had expected an uproar when he canceled the senior class trip, both parents and students seemed _____.
a. enraged
b. apathetic
c. suspicious
d. evasive

4. Make sure that drinking water is _____; otherwise, you could get sick.
a. valid
b. quenchable
c. impure
d. potable

5. I will vote in favor of the new city ordinance because it _____ many of the points we discussed earlier this year.
a. encompasses
b. releases
c. reminisces
d. disperses

6. Rachel _____ a plan to become a millionaire by age thirty.
a. devised
b. conformed
c. decreased
d. condoned

7. Joel ran away because he was _____ by the bully.
a. tolerated
b. disillusioned
c. consoled
d. intimidated

8. Robert was in a _____ about which tie to buy.
a. prestige
b. redundancy
c. quandary
d. deficit

9. Jessica needs an A in her class, so studying for exams takes _____ over watching the Academy Awards.
a. precedence
b. conformity
c. perplexity
d. endeavor

10. Jane wanted to be _____, so she wore her bright yellow dress with the pink bows to the picnic.
a. eminent
b. virtuous
c. conspicuous
d. obscure

11. Whitney fell asleep during the movie because it had a(n) _____ plot.
a. monotonous
b. torrid
c. ample
d. vital

12. Barney _____ to go back to school to study dog grooming.
  a. relied
  b. surmised
  c. presumed
  d. resolved

13. Your drawing is a fair _____ of my family as the infamous Doppler gang.
  a. portrayal
  b. council
  c. desolation
  d. degeneration

14. When Marty let go of the handlebars, his bike _____ down the hill and splashed into a duck pond.
  a. dissented
  b. ventilated
  c. careened
  d. agitated

15. My sister decided to change her diet when the sour milk on her cereal gave off a _____ odor.
  a. pungent
  b. virtuous
  c. fraudulent
  d. frugal

16. The five o'clock whistle _____ announces the end of the workday at the largest toothpaste factory in town.
  a. approvingly
  b. significantly
  c. symbolically
  d. audibly

17. Jade was so hungry after her workout that she _____ gobbled up the caviar.
  a. dynamically
  b. voraciously
  c. generously
  d. beneficially

18. A small _____ occurred when my car door nicked the fender of a neighboring motor scooter.
  a. mishap
  b. attraction
  c. reflex
  d. duplicate

PRACTICE 3

Choose the word that best fills the blank in the following sentences. Check your answers at the end of the lesson.

1. Columbus _____ believed that the world was round.
  a. optionally
  b. viciously
  c. prominently
  d. legitimately

2. Jeffrey was visibly nervous and spoke _____ about his upcoming appointment with his lawyer.
  a. warily
  b. luxuriously
  c. measurably
  d. narrowly

3. "I'm too young to date older men," Mandy said _____ when the high school senior asked her for a date.
   a. shapely
   b. coyly
   c. poorly
   d. totally

4. When Wayne found out that he had won the contest, he developed an _____ attitude, and we all had to listen to him crow about his accomplishments.
   a. arrogant
   b. achievable
   c. enlightened
   d. objective

5. Andrew showed _____ disregard for his pickup when he neglected to replenish the oil after the warning light came on.
   a. wanton
   b. admissive
   c. pretentious
   d. eloquent

6. Denise showed great _____ when she refused to discuss what was on the final exam in her economics class.
   a. substance
   b. generosity
   c. obligation
   d. integrity

7. The hail _____ the corn until the entire crop was lost.
   a. belittled
   b. pummeled
   c. rebuked
   d. commended

8. One of Angelo's _____ is collecting antique lemon juicers.
   a. eccentricities
   b. disappointments
   c. admonitions
   d. idioms

9. The motel offered a _____ after our long drive in the Grand Canyon.
   a. relapse
   b. respite
   c. brevity
   d. median

10. Margot brought large garbage bags to _____ our cleanup along Route 66.
    a. confound
    b. pacify
    c. integrate
    d. facilitate

11. Sandy's excellent bobsledding skills during the competition _____ what we all hoped to master.
    a. prevailed
    b. diverged
    c. exemplified
    d. varied

12. The _____ of sunshine and warm weather made for a happy vacation at the beach.
    a. assumption
    b. confluence
    c. seclusion
    d. treatise

13. Do you have the _____ papers to participate in the study on the effects of smoking?
   a. punitive
   b. grandiose
   c. restorative
   d. requisite

14. Don't _____ yourself: you must pass that exam to graduate.
   a. delude
   b. depreciate
   c. relinquish
   d. prohibit

15. When you write your paper about *The Catcher in the Rye*, please be sure to give a _____ description of the main character.
   a. principled
   b. determined
   c. comprehensive
   d. massive

16. Although Mary was _____ when we first met her, she soon came to talk more than any of us.
   a. customary
   b. reticent
   c. animated
   d. voluntary

17. Making money is a _____ to paying taxes.
   a. tedium
   b. precursor
   c. preference
   d. momentum

18. Stacy _____ told the press that she had accepted the nomination as board chairperson.
   a. repulsively
   b. reputedly
   c. perpetually
   d. principally

PRACTICE 4

Choose the word that best fills the blank in the following sentences. Check your answers at the end of the lesson.

1. After an hour of heavy rain, the storm _____ and we were able to get back out on the golf course.
   a. abated
   b. germinated
   c. constricted
   d. evoked

2. After years of experience, Wendy became the _____ veterinarian, performing surgery with ease.
   a. acute
   b. superficial
   c. consummate
   d. ample

3. Anthony tended his neighbors' goldfish _____ while they were on vacation.
   a. terminally
   b. perpendicularly
   c. assiduously
   d. essentially

4. The kinds of lurid, violent movies being produced now are a sad _____ society's morals.
  a. generalization about
  b. analysis of
  c. review of
  d. commentary on

5. The little Tyler boys got in trouble for _____ fish out of Mr. Crumm's pond.
  a. riling
  b. poaching
  c. provoking
  d. smuggling

6. The two cats could be _____ only by the number of rings on their tails; otherwise, they were exactly alike.
  a. separated
  b. divided
  c. disconnected
  d. differentiated

7. The room was _____, the bed unmade and the dishes dirty; mice and cockroaches were everywhere.
  a. squalid
  b. squeamish
  c. queasy
  d. licentious

8. The drive was dangerous because of the rain; on each slick, wet curve I was afraid we would _____ into a ditch.
  a. operate
  b. hydroplane
  c. submerge
  d. reconnoiter

9. Madame Zirantha was an experienced fortune-teller and _____, so she knew everything about the occult.
  a. dreamer
  b. comedian
  c. criminal
  d. clairvoyant

10. When Martha thought she saw a ghost in the corner of the room, she let out a(n) _____ shriek.
  a. unearthly
  b. covert
  c. abstruse
  d. esoteric

11. The tiny boat spun into the _____, and we were sure that all hope was lost for the lives of the sailors.
  a. matrix
  b. paradox
  c. vector
  d. vortex

12. The old man was _____; he refused to leave his home, even when told the volcano was about to erupt.
  a. recitative
  b. redundant
  c. repatriated
  d. recalcitrant

13. The project seemed _____, so we all applied ourselves to it with enthusiasm.
  a. implacable
  b. feasible
  c. incorrigible
  d. irreparable

14. The many colors in the swarm of butterflies seemed to create a(n) _____ cloud.
a. incandescent
b. iridescent
c. luminescent
d. cumulous

15. Mike and Jamal had perfect _____, each seeming to know, without being told, what the other felt.
a. stability
b. equilibrium
c. rapport
d. symmetry

16. In a(n) _____ voice, he told us all to sit down and be quiet.
a. clamorous
b. flocculent
c. affable
d. strident

17. Now that she is a teenager, my daughter is _____ to talk about virtually all personal topics—she simply sits and stares at me.
a. synchronous
b. unanimous
c. indentured
d. reticent

18. The *New York Times* printed an erroneous report about New York City student scores on standardized tests, so the school board demanded a(n) _____.
a. abolition
b. invalidation
c. retraction
d. annulment

19. Because the smoking gun was found in the defendant's hand as he bent over the body, his guilt is _____.
a. incomparable
b. inimitable
c. incontrovertible
d. inconspicuous

PRACTICE 5

Choose the word that best fills the blank in the following sentences. For each sentence you will have a pair of words to choose from. The pairs contain words that are easily confused and commonly misused.

1. Jane _____ first aid to the child with the broken arm.
a. administered
b. ministered

2. Enrique was _____ to see his kids after his long vacation.
a. eager
b. anxious

3. The judge set a huge amount for bail to _____ that the man would return to court.
a. ensure
b. insure

4. I turned green and became _____ after I rode the Super Loops ten times.
a. nauseous
b. nauseated

5. She looks fabulous in that dress; it fits
_____.
   a. good
   b. well

6. The United States is _____ of 50 states.
   a. composed
   b. comprised

7. If I lose all of my savings gambling in Las Vegas,
I will be profoundly _____.
   a. discomfited
   b. discomforted

8. All of the police officers were _____
witnesses because they actually saw the accident.
   a. credible
   b. credulous

9. His constant whistling _____ me like
nothing else does.
   a. annoys
   b. aggravates

10. Dogs _____ to the cold weather when
their fur grows thick.
   a. adapt
   b. adopt

11. A vitamin a day is part of a _____ diet.
   a. healthy
   b. healthful

12. If you see fit to _____ me into the hall
of fame, I will pay you for it.
   a. deduct
   b. induct

13. This book is an _____ study of the
Mayan culture.
   a. exhaustive
   b. exhausting

14. Because of her new baby it was not
_____ for Mary to attend her high
school reunion.
   a. feasible
   b. possible

15. The mail carrier _____ puts my
neighbor's mail in my box.
   a. continuously
   b. continually

16. We will _____ with the plan we made
earlier this month.
   a. proceed
   b. precede

17. Before buying a house you should seek the
_____ of a qualified attorney.
   a. counsel
   b. council

18. In most classes homework is _____.
   a. compulsive
   b. compulsory

19. Her students appreciate Professor Diamond's
_____ grading system.
   a. judicial
   b. judicious

20. Sam drove carefully on the _____
canyon road.
   a. tortuous
   b. torturous

ANSWERS

PRACTICE 1

1. **d.** The word *problem* in this context means a source of distress. Choices **b** and **c** do not make sense. Choice **a** is a great source of distress, but parking tickets are usually not a disaster.

2. **c.** *Rescue* in this context implies freeing from danger. The other choices do not make sense.

3. **a.** *Consider* means to think about carefully.

4. **b.** The context clue is "we knew nothing." *Secretive* means having the habit of keeping secrets.

5. **b.** *Summit* means the highest point, where the hikers would have a view.

6. **c.** A *consequence* is the result of something.

7. **c.** A *musty* odor is one that is stale or moldy. The other choices are not descriptive of an odor.

8. **a.** *Solitude*, unlike *loneliness* (choice **c**), can be a desirable thing. It's doubtful that a person who dealt with *crowds of noisy, demanding people* every day would want *association* (choice **b**). Choice **d** makes no sense.

9. **b.** To be *shunned* is to be avoided deliberately, usually as a punishment.

10. **c.** Bobby's acting up in class must have made Ms. Willy angry (*irate*) or she probably would not have thrown an eraser. Although she was certainly *animated* (choice **a**) and although throwing an eraser is *incautious* (choice **b**), these words do not imply anger. Choice **d** makes no sense.

11. **a.** *Spiteful* means filled with hate or malice.

12. **a.** *Accessible* means capable of being reached; being within reach.

13. **d.** *Outmoded* means or not longer in style or no longer usable.

14. **b.** A *quest* is a search or pursuit of something.

15. **d.** *Ingenious* means marked by originality, resourcefulness, and cleverness in conception; clever.

16. **c.** To be *indispensable* is to be essential or necessary.

17. **d.** *Chronic* means habitually reoccurring.

18. **b.** *Adversely* means acting against or in a contrary direction.

PRACTICE 2

1. **d.** *Docile* means easily led or managed.

2. **c.** *Explicit* means clearly defined.

3. **b.** *Apathetic* means having little or no concern. (The principal had expected an uproar, but that never happened.)

4. **d.** *Potable* means fit for drinking.

5. **a.** *Encompasses* in this context means includes.

6. **a.** *Devised* means to form in the mind by new combinations or applications of ideas or principles; to plan to obtain or bring about.

7. **d.** To *intimidate* means to make timid or fearful; to frighten.

8. **c.** *Quandary* means a state of perplexity or doubt.

9. **a.** *Precedence* means priority of importance—i.e., studying is more important to Jessica than watching the Academy Awards.

10. **c.** *Conspicuous* means obvious to the eye or mind; attracting attention.

11. **a.** *Monotonous* means having a tedious sameness.

12. **d.** *Resolved* means having reached a firm decision about something.

13. **a.** *Portrayal* means representation or portrait.

14. **c.** *Careen* means to rush headlong or carelessly; to lurch or swerve while in motion.

15. **a.** *Pungent* implies a sharp, stinging, or biting quality, especially of odor.

16. **d.** *Audibly* means heard or the manner of being heard.

17. **b.** *Voraciously* means having a huge appetite; ravenously.

18. **a.** *Mishap* means an unfortunate accident.

PRACTICE 3

1. **d.** *Legitimately* means in a manner conforming to recognized principles or accepted rules or standards.

2. **a.** *Warily* means in a manner marked by keen caution, cunning, and watchful prudence. The context clue in this sentence is Jeffrey's nervousness.

3. **b.** *Coyly* means in a manner that is marked by cute, coquettish, or artful playfulness. In this context, the other choices make no sense.

4. **a.** *Arrogant* means exaggerating or disposed to exaggerate one's own worth or importance in an overbearing manner.

5. **a.** *Wanton* means being without check or limitation.

6. **d.** *Integrity* means firm adherence to a code of moral values; honesty.

7. **b.** To *pummel* means to pound or beat.

8. **a.** An *eccentricity* is something that deviates from the norm. (Antique lemon juicers are not a commonplace item.)

9. **b.** *Respite* means an interval of rest and relief.

10. **d.** *Facilitate* means to make easier or help to bring about.

11. **c.** *Exemplify* means to be an instance of or serve as an example.

12. **b.** *Confluence* means a coming or flowing together, meeting, or gathering at one point.

13. **d.** *Requisite* means essential or necessary.

14. **a.** *Delude* means to mislead the mind; to deceive.

15. **c.** *Comprehensive* means covering completely or broadly. (*Massive*, choice **d**, refers to a large or bulky mass.)

16. **b.** *Reticent* means inclined to be silent or uncommunicative; reserved. Mary was silent at first, but then talked more than anyone else.

17. **b.** *Precursor* means something that comes before.

18. **b.** *Reputedly* means according to general belief.

PRACTICE 4

1. **a.** *Abated* means to decrease in force or intensity.

2. **c.** *Consummate* means extremely skilled and experienced.

3. **c.** *Assiduously* means in a careful manner or with unremitting attention.

4. **d.** A *commentary* is something that explains or illustrates and fits best in this context.

5. **b.** To *poach* is to trespass on another's property in order to steal fish or game. Choices **a** and **c** would make little sense. Choice **d** seems too grand a description for the actions of two small boys.

6. d. To *differentiate* between two things is to establish the distinction between them. The other choices, although somewhat related, make no sense.

7. a. Something *squalid* has a dirty or wretched appearance. The other adjectives, though somewhat related, can properly be applied to a person but not to a place.

8. b. When a car goes out of control and skims along the surface of a wet road, it is called *hydroplaning*.

9. d. A *clairvoyant* is someone who can perceive matters beyond the range of ordinary perception.

10. a. The word *unearthly* (frighteningly weird and unnatural) best describes the way someone might shriek when they see a ghost. A shriek cannot be *covert* (hidden, choice **b**), nor can it be *abstruse* (difficult to understand, choice **c**) because it does not seek to explain anything. The word *esoteric* (known only to a small number) does not precisely apply to a *shriek*, either.

11. d. A *vortex* is a whirlpool and so fits the sentence. The other choices do not make sense.

12. d. To be *recalcitrant* is to be stubbornly resistant. The other adjectives are not usually applied to human beings.

13. b. To be *feasible* is to be practicable and so the word best fits this sentence. The other three choices would not apply to projects that are possible (note that they all begin with prefixes generally meaning "not").

14. b. Something that is *iridescent* displays lustrous, rainbow colors. Choices **a** and **b** are somewhat close, but neither necessarily includes color as a necessary property.

Cumulous (choice **d**) is a scientific name for a type of cloud.

15. c. To have *rapport* is to have mutual trust and emotional affinity. The other words do not necessarily imply trust.

16. d. A *strident* voice is one that is loud, harsh, and grating, so it best fits the sentiment "sit down and shut up." The word *clamorous* (choice **a**) has the connotation of a public outcry in more than one voice. *Flocculent* (choice **b**) denotes something fluffy or woolly, and *affable* (choice **c**) means "amiable."

17. d. To be *reticent* is to be disinclined to speak out. The other choices make no sense in this context.

18. c. To *retract* something is to take it back or disavow it. This is the term usually applied to disavowing something erroneous or libelous printed in a newspaper. The other choices are somewhat similar in meaning but do not normally apply to newspaper errors.

19. c. If something is *incontrovertible*, it is irrefutable. This word makes most sense in the context of an obvious crime.

PRACTICE 5

1. a. To *administer* means to give something remedially (transitive verb). To *minister* means to aid or give service to people (intransitive verb).

2. a. *Eager* implies enthusiastic or impatient desire or interest. *Anxious* implies a more negative feeling: an extreme uneasiness of mind, or worried.

3. **a.** *Ensure* means to make a future occurrence certain or reliable; *insure* means protecting the worth of goods; *assure* means to promise or cause someone to count on.

4. **b.** *Nauseated* means to feel nausea or the condition of feeling sick. *Nauseous* means causing nausea; nauseating; sickening. If you say you are nauseous it means you have unpleasant powers.

5. **b.** *Well* should be used as an adverb to modify verbs (how does it fit?). *Good* is an adjective often used with linking verbs (be, seem, or appear).

6. **b.** *Comprised* means to consist of—it expresses the relation of the larger to the smaller (think of this larger sense by remembering that *comprised* is a longer word than composes). *Composed* means to make up the parts of.

7. **a.** *Discomfit* means to wholly undo or defeat. *Discomfort* means to deprive of comfort or to distress.

8. **a.** *Credible* means offering reasonable grounds for being believed; *credulous* means ready to believe, especially on slight or uncertain evidence.

9. **a.** *Annoy* means a wearing on the nerves by persistent petty unpleasantness; *aggravate* means to make worse, more serious, or more severe—to intensify unpleasantly.

10. **a.** *Adapt* implies a modification according to changing circumstances. *Adopt* means accepting something created by another or foreign to one's nature.

11. **b.** *Healthful* implies a positive contribution to a healthy condition, or beneficial to health. *Healthy* implies full of strength and vigor as well as freedom from signs of disease.

12. **b.** *Induct* means to introduce or initiate. *Deduct* means to take away from a total.

13. **a.** *Exhaustive* means treating all parts without omission. *Exhausting* means tiring.

14. **a.** *Feasible* means logical or likely. *Possible* means capable of happening or existing.

15. **b.** *Continuously* means uninterrupted in time. *Continually* means recurring regularly.

16. **a.** *Proceed* means to go forward in an orderly way; *precede* means to come before.

17. **a.** *Counsel* means advice or guidance. A *council* is an assembly of people called together for consultation.

18. **b.** *Compulsory* means obligatory or required. *Compulsive* means having the capacity to compel.

19. **a.** *Judicious* is having or exhibiting sound judgment. *Judicial* is of, or relating to, courts of law.

20. **a.** *Tortuous* means winding or twisting. *Torturous* means of, relating to, or causing torture.

L·E·S·S·O·N

SYNONYMS AND ANTONYMS

14

A word is a synonym of another word if it has the same or nearly the same meaning as the word to which it is being compared. An antonym is a word that means the opposite of the word to which it is being compared. Questions on the ASVAB often ask you to find the synonym or antonym of a word. Sometimes the word will be in context—surrounded by a sentence that helps you guess what the word means. Other times, you'll just get the word and have to figure out what the word means without any help from the context.

SYNONYMS

Questions that ask for synonyms can be tricky because they require you to recognize the meanings of several words that may be unfamiliar to you—not only the words in the question, but also the words in the answer choices. Usually, the best strategy is to look at the structure of the word and listen for its sound. See if a part of a word looks familiar. Think of other words you know that may have similar key elements and then think about how those words could be related.

PRACTICE 1

For each question, choose the synonym. Check your answers at the end of the lesson.

1. Which word means the same as ENTHUSIASTIC?
   a. adamant
   b. available
   c. cheerful
   d. eager

2. Which word means the same as ADEQUATE?
   a. sufficient
   b. mediocre
   c. proficient
   d. average

3. Which word means the same as ECSTATIC?
   a. inconsistent
   b. positive
   c. wild
   d. thrilled

4. Which word means the same as AFFECT?
   a. accomplish
   b. cause
   c. sicken
   d. influence

5. Which word means the same as CONTINUOUS?
   a. intermittent
   b. adjacent
   c. uninterrupted
   d. contiguous

6. Which word means the same as COURTESY?
   a. civility
   b. congruity
   c. conviviality
   d. rudeness

7. Which word means the same as FRAIL?
   a. vivid
   b. delicate
   c. robust
   d. adaptable

8. Which word means the same as RECUPERATE?
   a. mend
   b. endorse
   c. persist
   d. worsen

9. Which word means the same as SUFFICIENT?
   a. majestic
   b. scarce
   c. tranquil
   d. adequate

10. Which word means the same as COMPOSURE?
    a. agitation
    b. poise
    c. liveliness
    d. stimulation

11. Which word means the same as ECCENTRIC?
    a. normal
    b. frugal
    c. peculiar
    d. selective

12. Which word means the same as COMMENDABLE?
    a. admirable
    b. accountable
    c. irresponsible
    d. noticeable

13. Which word means the same as PASSIVE?

    a. inactive

    b. emotional

    c. lively

    d. woeful

14. Which word means the same as VAST?

    a. attentive

    b. immense

    c. steady

    d. slight

15. Which word means the same as COMPLY?

    a. subdue

    b. entertain

    c. flatter

    d. obey

16. Which word means the same as WILL?

    a. resolve

    b. spite

    c. sanity

    d. idleness

17. Which word means the same as ENLIGHTEN?

    a. relocate

    b. confuse

    c. comply

    d. teach

18. Which word means the same as RIGOROUS?

    a. demanding

    b. tolerable

    c. lenient

    d. disorderly

19. Which word means the same as OBLIVIOUS?

    a. visible

    b. sinister

    c. conscious

    d. unaware

20. Which word means the same as VERIFY?

    a. disclose

    b. confirm

    c. refute

    d. unite

PRACTICE 2

For each question, choose the synonym. Check your answers at the end of the lesson.

1. Which word means the same as ERRONEOUS?

    a. digressive

    b. confused

    c. impenetrable

    d. incorrect

2. Which word means the same as GROTESQUE?

    a. extreme

    b. frenzied

    c. hideous

    d. typical

3. Which word means the same as GARBLED?

    a. lucid

    b. unintelligible

    c. devoured

    d. outrageous

4. Which word means the same as EXPOSE?

    a. relate

    b. develop

    c. reveal

    d. pretend

5. Which word means the same as COERCE?
   a. force
   b. permit
   c. waste
   d. deny

6. Which word means the same as ABRUPT?
   a. interrupt
   b. sudden
   c. extended
   d. corrupt

7. Which word means the same as APATHY?
   a. hostility
   b. depression
   c. indifference
   d. concern

8. Which word means the same as DESPAIR?
   a. mourning
   b. disregard
   c. hopelessness
   d. loneliness

9. Which word means the same as CONTEMPTUOUS?
   a. respectful
   b. unique
   c. scornful
   d. insecure

10. Which word means the same as TOTE?
   a. acquire
   b. carry
   c. tremble
   d. abandon

11. Which word means the same as DISTINCT?
   a. satisfied
   b. frenzied
   c. uneasy
   d. separate

12. Which word means the same as FLAGRANT?
   a. secret
   b. worthless
   c. noble
   d. glaring

13. Which word means the same as ORATION?
   a. nuisance
   b. independence
   c. address
   d. length

14. Which word means the same as LIBEL?
   a. description
   b. praise
   c. destiny
   d. slander

15. Which word means the same as PHILANTHROPY?
   a. selfishness
   b. fascination
   c. disrespect
   d. generosity

16. Which word means the same as PROXIMITY?
   a. distance
   b. agreement
   c. nearness
   d. intelligence

17. Which word means the same as NEGLIGIBLE?
 a. insignificant
 b. delicate
 c. meaningful
 d. illegible

18. Which word means the same as VIGILANT?
 a. nonchalant
 b. watchful
 c. righteous
 d. strenuous

19. Which word means the same as ASTUTE?
 a. perceptive
 b. inattentive
 c. stubborn
 d. elegant

20. Which word means the same as COLLABORATE?
 a. cooperate
 b. coordinate
 c. entice
 d. elaborate

Practice 3

For each question, choose the word that has the same or nearly the same meaning as the capitalized word. Check your answers at the end of the lesson.

1. JOURNAL
 a. trip
 b. receipt
 c. diary
 d. list

2. OPPORTUNITY
 a. sensitivity
 b. arrogance
 c. chance
 d. reference

3. INVENT
 a. insert
 b. discover
 c. apply
 d. allow

4. SPHERE
 a. air
 b. spread
 c. globe
 d. enclosure

5. REFINE
 a. condone
 b. provide
 c. change
 d. purify

6. PLEDGE
 a. picture
 b. idea
 c. quote
 d. promise

7. GANGLY
 a. illegally
 b. closely
 c. ugly
 d. lanky

8. SAGE
 a. wise
 b. obnoxious
 c. conceited
 d. heartless

9. NAVIGATE
 a. search
 b. decide
 c. steer
 d. assist

10. DORMANT
 a. hidden
 b. slumbering
 c. rigid
 d. misplaced

11. BANISH
 a. exile
 b. decorate
 c. succumb
 d. encourage

12. TAILOR
 a. measure
 b. construct
 c. launder
 d. alter

13. YIELD
 a. merge
 b. relinquish
 c. destroy
 d. hinder

14. CROON
 a. swim
 b. vocalize
 c. stroke
 d. yell

15. ETERNAL
 a. timeless
 b. heavenly
 c. loving
 d. wealthy

16. HOSTEL
 a. turnstile
 b. cot
 c. trek
 d. inn

17. STOW
 a. pack
 b. curtsy
 c. fool
 d. trample

18. MESA
 a. brain
 b. plateau
 c. wagon
 d. dwelling

19. ADO
 a. idiom
 b. punishment
 c. cost
 d. fuss

20. INTIMATE
 a. frightening
 b. curious
 c. private
 d. characteristic

PRACTICE 4

Choose the word that means the same or nearly the same as the underlined word. Check your answers at the end of the lesson.

1. its <u>inferior</u> quality
   a. noted
   b. distinguished
   c. lower
   d. questionable

2. in a <u>curt</u> manner
   a. gruff
   b. careful
   c. devious
   d. calm

3. their <u>perilous</u> journey
   a. dangerous
   b. doubtful
   c. adventurous
   d. thrilling

4. the <u>precise</u> amount
   a. fair
   b. exact
   c. undetermined
   d. valuable

5. to <u>commence</u> the meeting
   a. begin
   b. leave
   c. disclose
   d. terminate

6. a <u>humble</u> person
   a. common
   b. tolerant
   c. conceited
   d. meek

7. a <u>jubilant</u> graduate
   a. charming
   b. joyful
   c. stubborn
   d. scholarly

8. created a <u>replica</u>
   a. portion
   b. masterpiece
   c. prompt
   d. copy

9. a <u>temperate</u> climate
   a. moderate
   b. harsh
   c. warm
   d. cold

10. a <u>destitute</u> family
    a. poor
    b. wise
    c. traveling
    d. large

11. the <u>agile</u> dancer
    a. proud
    b. nimble
    c. humble
    d. talented

12. acted <u>brazenly</u>
    a. boldly
    b. blissfully
    c. brutally
    d. broadly

13. the <u>unique</u> individual
    a. rigorous
    b. admirable
    c. unparalleled
    d. remarkable

14. the <u>prerequisite</u> number of items
    a. optional
    b. preferred
    c. advisable
    d. required

15. <u>alleviate</u> the pain
    a. ease
    b. tolerate
    c. stop
    d. intensify

16. <u>inundated</u> with requests
    a. provided
    b. bothered
    c. rewarded
    d. flooded

17. the <u>unanimous</u> decision
    a. uniform
    b. divided
    c. adamant
    d. clear-cut

18. the <u>proficient</u> worker
    a. inexperienced
    b. unequaled
    c. efficient
    d. skilled

19. <u>obstinately</u> refused
    a. repeatedly
    b. reluctantly
    c. angrily
    d. stubbornly

20. to <u>rectify</u> the situation
    a. correct
    b. forget
    c. alter
    d. abuse

PRACTICE 5

Choose the word that means the same or nearly the same as the underlined word. Check your answers at the end of the lesson.

1. <u>expedite</u> the process
    a. accelerate
    b. evaluate
    c. reverse
    d. justify

2. reversal of <u>fortune</u>
    a. luck
    b. status
    c. action
    d. thought

3. to <u>absolve</u> a person
    a. convict
    b. accuse
    c. forgive
    d. exclude

4. to <u>hoist</u> the flag
    a. lower
    b. destroy
    c. salute
    d. raise

5. the <u>predictable</u> outcome
    a. worrisome
    b. unexpected
    c. unfavorable
    d. foreseeable

6. to <u>shore up</u> a house
    a. demolish
    b. renovate
    c. support
    d. remodel

7. <u>simmering</u> anger
   a. unacknowledged
   b. diminishing
   c. righteous
   d. seething

8. to <u>initiate</u> a campaign
   a. support
   b. begin
   c. sabotage
   d. run

9. <u>ravenous</u> hunger
   a. natural
   b. ungratified
   c. voracious
   d. satisfied

10. <u>uninhabitable</u> island
   a. deserted
   b. unlivable
   c. remote
   d. uncivilized

11. <u>suppressed</u> anger
   a. explosive
   b. repressed
   c. minimized
   d. expressed

12. to be <u>immersed in</u> study
   a. trapped in
   b. absorbed in
   c. learning through
   d. enriched by

13. <u>secular</u> music
   a. non-religious
   b. atheistic
   c. religious
   d. ancient

14. to <u>haggle</u> over the price
   a. bargain
   b. complain
   c. worry
   d. cheat

15. <u>palpable</u> tension
   a. rising
   b. understated
   c. nervous
   d. tangible

16. to get <u>a vicarious</u> thrill
   a. a dangerous
   b. a forbidden
   c. an imaginary
   d. a secretive

17. urban <u>sprawl</u>
   a. decay
   b. development
   c. haphazard growth
   d. increase in crime

18. an <u>exotic</u> land
   a. foreign and intriguing
   b. alien and frightening
   c. ludicrous and amusing
   d. remote and boring

19. a <u>meandering</u> stream
   a. clear
   b. flowing
   c. polluted
   d. winding

20. a <u>precarious</u> situation
   a. joyous
   b. dangerous
   c. unforgettable
   d. secure

ANTONYMS

Many antonyms seem obvious—good and bad, night and day—but others are not as easily recognizable. This is because many words have more than one meaning. For example, the word *clear* could mean cloudless, or transparent, or unmistakable. For each of those meanings, clear has an opposite. If an antonym isn't obvious, think about other possible meanings of the word. Also, don't be fooled by answer choices that are synonyms. Remember that you are looking for a word that means the opposite, not a word that means the same. You can check your answers at the end of the lesson.

PRACTICE 6

1. Which word means the *opposite* of UNITY?
   a. discord
   b. stimulation
   c. consent
   d. neglect

2. Which word means the *opposite* of DETEST?
   a. prohibit
   b. hate
   c. examine
   d. admire

3. Which word means the *opposite* of VALIANT?
   a. instinctive
   b. cowardly
   c. cynical
   d. worthy

4. Which word means the *opposite* of LENIENT?
   a. capable
   b. impractical
   c. merciful
   d. domineering

5. Which word means the *opposite* of TARNISH?
   a. absorb
   b. endure
   c. shine
   d. sully

6. Which word means the *opposite* of MANDATORY?
   a. apparent
   b. equal
   c. optional
   d. required

7. Which word means the *opposite* of CHAGRIN?
   a. conviction
   b. irritation
   c. pleasure
   d. humanity

8. Which word means the *opposite* of COMMENCE?
   a. initiate
   b. adapt
   c. harass
   d. terminate

9. Which word means the *opposite* of CONSCIENTIOUS?
   a. careless
   b. apologetic
   c. diligent
   d. boisterous

10. Which word means the *opposite* of DEFICIENT?
    a. necessary
    b. complete
    c. flawed
    d. simple

11. Which word means the *opposite* of CLARIFY?
    a. explain
    b. dismay
    c. obscure
    d. provide

12. Which word means the *opposite* of GRANT?
    a. deny
    b. consume
    c. allocate
    d. provoke

13. Which word means the *opposite* of LUCID?
    a. ordinary
    b. turbulent
    c. implausible
    d. unclear

14. Which word means the *opposite* of IMPARTIAL?
    a. complete
    b. prejudiced
    c. unbiased
    d. erudite

15. Which word means the *opposite* of JUDICIOUS?
    a. partial
    b. litigious
    c. imprudent
    d. unrestrained

16. Which word means the *opposite* of DISSONANCE?
    a. harmony
    b. carefulness
    c. specificity
    d. value

17. Which word means the *opposite* of ERUDITE?
    a. uneducated
    b. polite
    c. unknown
    d. agitated

18. Which word means the *opposite* of AMIABLE?
    a. dangerous
    b. permissive
    c. aloof
    d. congenial

19. Which word means the *opposite* of COMPETENT?
    a. incomplete
    b. intense
    c. incapable
    d. massive

20. Which word means the *opposite* of PROMOTE?
    a. explicate
    b. curtail
    c. concede
    d. retain

PRACTICE 7

Choose the word that means the OPPOSITE or most nearly the opposite of the word in capitals.

1. REQUIREMENT
    a. plan
    b. consequence
    c. option
    d. accident

2. IRRITATE
   a. soothe
   b. drain
   c. resist
   d. solve

3. PUNCTUAL
   a. random
   b. smooth
   c. intermittent
   d. tardy

4. VIRTUE
   a. reality
   b. fact
   c. vice
   d. amateur

5. HARMONY
   a. noise
   b. brevity
   c. safety
   d. discord

6. INSULT
   a. compliment
   b. contempt
   c. argument
   d. attitude

7. GENERAL
   a. specific
   b. total
   c. insignificant
   d. substantial

8. FORTUNATE
   a. excluded
   b. hapless
   c. hardworking
   d. lucky

9. IMAGINARY
   a. sober
   b. ordinary
   c. unrealistic
   d. factual

10. DEMOLISH
    a. attend
    b. consider
    c. create
    d. stifle

11. NOTABLE
    a. oral
    b. graceful
    c. legal
    d. ordinary

12. PRIM
    a. outrageous
    b. last
    c. ugly
    d. cantankerous

13. PROSPEROUS
    a. affluent
    b. destitute
    c. cowardly
    d. receptive

14. ABSORB
    a. acquire
    b. repel
    c. consume
    d. assist

15. CRITICAL
    a. inimical
    b. judgmental
    c. massive
    d. trivial

16. NIMBLE
   a. sturdy
   b. sluggish
   c. thoughtless
   d. relaxed

17. TRANQUIL
   a. agitated
   b. explicit
   c. sluggish
   d. composed

18. SPRIGHTLY
   a. eagerly
   b. loftily
   c. dully
   d. locally

19. INFANTILE
   a. despicable
   b. adolescent
   c. mature
   d. perpetual

20. IMPULSIVE
   a. secure
   b. mandatory
   c. rash
   d. cautious

PRACTICE 8

Choose the word that means the OPPOSITE or most nearly the opposite of the word in capitals.

1. PRUDENT
   a. rash
   b. licentious
   c. libertine
   d. demonstrative

2. RETAIN
   a. withhold
   b. release
   c. succumb
   d. incise

3. SCANT
   a. pellucid
   b. meager
   c. copious
   d. vocal

4. STEADFAST
   a. envious
   b. fickle
   c. improvident
   d. sluggish

5. STRINGENT
   a. obese
   b. lax
   c. obtuse
   d. fluid

6. SUBJECTIVE
   a. invective
   b. objectionable
   c. unbiased
   d. obedient

7. SUCCINCT
   a. distinct
   b. laconic
   c. unpersuasive
   d. verbose

8. TEDIOUS
   a. stimulating
   b. alarming
   c. intemperate
   d. tranquil

9. UNIFORM
   a. dissembling
   b. diverse
   c. bizarre
   d. slovenly

10. WARY
   a. alert
   b. leery
   c. worried
   d. careless

11. NOVEL
   a. dangerous
   b. unsettled
   c. suitable
   d. old

12. FALLACY
   a. truth
   b. blessing
   c. weakness
   d. fable

13. EXONERATE
   a. minimize
   b. respect
   c. irritate
   d. blame

14. SUBSEQUENT
   a. necessary
   b. insignificant
   c. primary
   d. previous

15. NONCHALANT
   a. intelligent
   b. popular
   c. concerned
   d. reckless

16. EXCISE
   a. sleep
   b. retain
   c. organize
   d. staple

17. DISPERSE
   a. gather
   b. agree
   c. praise
   d. satisfy

18. PREVARICATION
   a. ignorance
   b. veracity
   c. courtesy
   d. serenity

19. MIRTH
   a. height
   b. solemnity
   c. expense
   d. preparation

20. LIBERATE
   a. conserve
   b. restrain
   c. attack
   d. ruin

21. FALTERING
  a. steady
  b. adoring
  c. explanatory
  d. reluctant

22. OPTIMUM
  a. mediocre
  b. victorious
  c. worst
  d. rational

23. EPHEMERAL
  a. internal
  b. enduring
  c. temporary
  d. hidden

PRACTICE 9

Choose the word that means the OPPOSITE or most nearly the opposite of the word in capitals.

1. ORIENT
  a. confuse
  b. arouse
  c. deter
  d. simplify

2. LEVITATE
  a. plod
  b. undulate
  c. whisper
  d. sink

3. PACIFY
  a. complicate
  b. dismiss
  c. excite
  d. atomize

4. PLAUSIBLE
  a. insufficient
  b. apologetic
  c. unbelievable
  d. credible

5. AVIDLY
  a. partially
  b. unenthusiastically
  c. equally
  d. unkindly

6. MEEKLY
  a. mildly
  b. painfully
  c. forcefully
  d. politely

7. COMPLACENT
  a. concerned
  b. pleasant
  c. happy
  d. convinced

8. AMBIGUOUS
  a. apathetic
  b. certain
  c. equivocal
  d. indefinite

9. ESTEEM
  a. disrespect
  b. disregard
  c. dissent
  d. disabuse

10. ELOQUENT
   a. shabby
   b. fluent
   c. inarticulate
   d. plain

11. DETERRENT
   a. encouragement
   b. obstacle
   c. proponent
   d. discomfort

12. HIERARCHICAL
   a. monarchical
   b. oligarchical
   c. placid
   d. egalitarian

13. IMPERTINENT
   a. animated
   b. rude
   c. relentless
   d. polite

14. LUDICROUS
   a. absurd
   b. somber
   c. reasonable
   d. charitable

15. ARCHAIC
   a. tangible
   b. modern
   c. ancient
   d. haunted

16. SULLEN
   a. morose
   b. impetuous
   c. provocative
   d. jovial

17. AWE
   a. contempt
   b. reverence
   c. valor
   d. distortion

18. TAUT
   a. neutral
   b. relaxed
   c. rigid
   d. vague

19. RILE
   a. appease
   b. prosper
   c. oppress
   d. irk

20. MAR
   a. delineate
   b. bolster
   c. clarify
   d. repair

21. SKEPTIC
   a. innovator
   b. friend
   c. politician
   d. believer

22. PREDECESSOR
   a. successor
   b. antecedent
   c. descendant
   d. ancestor

23. HYPOTHETICAL
   a. uncritical
   b. actual
   c. specific
   d. imaginary

24. ENHANCE
    a. diminish
    b. improve
    c. digress
    d. deprive

PRACTICE 10

Choose the word that means the OPPOSITE or most nearly the opposite of the word in capitals.

1. INTREPID
    a. belligerent
    b. consistent
    c. chivalrous
    d. fearful

2. METHODICAL
    a. erratic
    b. deliberate
    c. hostile
    d. deformed

3. LATENT
    a. slow
    b. tardy
    c. dormant
    d. active

4. AFFABLE
    a. disagreeable
    b. hollow
    c. simple
    d. eager

5. TREPIDATION
    a. distribution
    b. agitation
    c. fearlessness
    d. uniformity

6. AUSPICIOUS
    a. unpromising
    b. repulsive
    c. jealous
    d. inattentive

7. MILITANT
    a. expeditious
    b. judicious
    c. pacifistic
    d. creative

8. FURTIVELY
    a. silently
    b. openly
    c. mildly
    d. quickly

9. ENTICE
    a. excite
    b. tempt
    c. express
    d. repel

10. INGENUOUS
    a. useful
    b. infinite
    c. calculating
    d. immature

11. OSTENTATIOUS
    a. hilarious
    b. humble
    c. careful
    d. obnoxious

12. ENDORSE
   a. condemn
   b. recommend
   c. announce
   d. adopt

13. ACCEDE
   a. excel
   b. retard
   c. disapprove
   d. increase

14. COPIOUS
   a. redundant
   b. meager
   c. ample
   d. shy

15. AMBIVALENCE
   a. compensation
   b. decisiveness
   c. enthusiasm
   d. devotion

16. DIVERGENT
   a. persuasive
   b. identical
   c. incomplete
   d. malicious

17. PENSIVE
   a. nervous
   b. prejudiced
   c. dizzy
   d. thoughtless

18. DISCERNIBLE
   a. invisible
   b. recognizable
   c. paradoxical
   d. scornful

19. VACILLATE
   a. struggle
   b. bleed
   c. resolve
   d. liberate

20. ABHOR
   a. scare
   b. surprise
   c. desire
   d. inspire

21. CHORTLE
   a. rhyme
   b. moan
   c. gravel
   d. guess

22. RAUCOUS
   a. ambitious
   b. continuous
   c. significant
   d. calm

23. DEPLETE
   a. report
   b. conform
   c. replace
   d. revise

24. EQUANIMITY
   a. excellence
   b. judgment
   c. compatibility
   d. perplexity

ANSWERS

PRACTICE 1

1. **d.** *Enthusiastic* means eager or excited.
2. **a.** If something is *adequate,* it is sufficient.
3. **d.** A person who is *ecstatic* is thrilled or exhilarated.
4. **d.** To *affect* means to influence.
5. **c.** *Continuous* means marked by uninterrupted extension in space and time.
6. **a.** A *courtesy* implies being courteous or mannerly; it is civility.
7. **b.** A *frail* person is weak and delicate.
8. **a.** *Recuperate* means to heal; to mend.
9. **d.** *Sufficient* and *adequate* both mean enough.
10. **b.** If you gain your *composure,* you have poise.
11. **c.** An *eccentric* person is considered to be peculiar.
12. **a.** *Commendable* is the same as admirable.
13. **a.** *Passive* means not active.
14. **b.** *Vast* means very great in size; immense.
15. **d.** To *comply* is the same as to obey.
16. **a.** *Will* and *resolve* mean the same thing.
17. **d.** If you *enlighten* someone, you have taught them something.
18. **a.** If something is *rigorous,* it is demanding.
19. **d.** If you are *oblivious* to your surroundings, you are unaware of them.
20. **b.** To *verify* means to establish the truth or accuracy; to confirm.

PRACTICE 2

1. **d.** *Erroneous* means inaccurate, faulty, or incorrect.
2. **c.** *Grotesque* means freakish, distorted, or hideous.
3. **b.** If something is *garbled,* it is jumbled or unintelligible.
4. **c.** If you *expose* something, you reveal it.
5. **a.** To *coerce* means to dominate by force.
6. **b.** *Abrupt* means sudden, quick, or hasty.
7. **c.** *Apathy* means a lack of interest or concern; indifference.
8. **c.** *Despair* means utter loss of hope.
9. **c.** A *contemptuous* person is full of scorn.
10. **b.** To *tote* means to carry.
11. **d.** If something is *distinct* it is distinguishable, or separate.
12. **d.** *Flagrant* means glaringly offensive.
13. **c.** An *oration* is a speech; an address.
14. **d.** *Libel* and *slander* both refer to defaming someone.
15. **d.** *Philanthropy* is a noun that means goodwill toward fellowmen; humanitarianism; generosity.
16. **c.** *Proximity* means the state of being proximate or near.
17. **a.** *Negligible* means of little consequence; insignificant.
18. **b.** *Vigilant* means watchful, especially to danger.
19. **a.** *Astute* and *perceptive* both mean having or showing a keen awareness.
20. **a.** To *collaborate* means to work jointly with others; to cooperate.

PRACTICE 3

1. **c.** A *journal* and a *diary* are both records of daily happenings.
2. **c.** An *opportunity* to do something is the same as a *chance* to do it.
3. **b.** *Invent* means to create or to *discover.*
4. **c.** *Sphere* and *globe* both mean ball or orb.

5. **d.** To *refine* and to *purify* both mean to remove impurities.

6. **d.** *Pledge* and *promise* both mean a declaration that one will do something.

7. **d.** *Gangly* and *lanky* both mean tall, thin, and awkward.

8. **a.** *Sage* and *wise* both mean intelligent, perceptive.

9. **c.** To *navigate* and to *steer* both mean to direct a course.

10. **b.** *Dormant* and *slumbering* both mean sleeping.

11. **a.** To *banish* and to *exile* both mean to force to leave.

12. **d.** To *tailor* and to *alter* both mean to make something fit.

13. **b.** To *yield* and to *relinquish* both mean to give up.

14. **b.** To *croon* and to *vocalize* both mean to sing.

15. **a.** *Eternal* and *timeless* both mean without end.

16. **d.** A *hostel* and an *inn* are both lodging places.

17. **a.** To *stow* and to *pack* both mean to store away.

18. **b.** A *mesa* and a *plateau* are both hills with flat tops.

19. **d.** *Ado* and *fuss,* when used as nouns, both mean a hubbub or commotion.

20. **c.** *Intimate* and *private* both mean personal.

PRACTICE 4

1. **c.** *Inferior* is lower in rank, quality, or importance.

2. **a.** *Curt* means in a rude or *gruff* manner.

3. **a.** *Perilous* means in a hazardous manner; dangerous.

4. **b.** *Precise* means exactly or sharply defined.

5. **a.** *Commence* means begin.

6. **d.** Someone who is *humble* is meek and non-assertive.

7. **b.** *Jubilant* means joyful.

8. **d.** A *replica* is a close reproduction; a copy or duplicate.

9. **a.** *Temperate* means not extreme or excessive; *moderate* means avoiding extremes of behavior or expression.

10. **a.** *Destitute* means lacking possessions and resources.

11. **b.** *Agile* means marked by ready ability to move with quick and easy grace; *nimble* means quick and light in motion.

12. **a.** *Brazenly* means marked by contemptuous boldness.

13. **c.** *Unique* means being the only one of its kind; *unparalleled* means unequaled.

14. **d.** To be a *prerequisite* is to be required; to be *required* is to be needed.

15. **a.** To *alleviate* is to make more bearable; to *ease* is to free from pain.

16. **d.** To be *inundated* is to be overwhelmed or swamped; to be *flooded* is to be submerged.

17. **a.** *Unanimous* means in complete assent or agreement; *uniform* means unvarying or the same as another or others.

18. **d.** To be *proficient* is to be expert or adept at something; to be *skilled* is to show ability or expertness.

19. **d.** *Obstinately* means refractory or stubborn; *stubbornly* means unduly determined, not easily persuaded.

20. **a.** To *rectify* is to set something right; to *correct* is to remove errors from something.

CONTENTS

INTRODUCTION

Already, you're a giant leap ahead.

If you're thinking of joining the military, and have picked up this book to prepare for the ASVAB exam, you're a giant leap ahead of people who will take the ASVAB, but will not study for it. Every person who enlists in the Army, Navy, Air Force, or Marines must take the Armed Services Vocational Battery (ASVAB). But not every person who takes the test is wise enough to *prepare*.

Make no mistake: When you join the military, you're competing for a limited number of jobs. The better you score on the ASVAB, the more job choices will be open to you. The fact you're preparing for the exam increases your chances of landing a military job that will reward you both during a service career and in a great civilian job after you leave the military.

This introduction will answer several ASVAB FAQs (Frequently Asked Questions):

- what the ASVAB is, exactly
- what kinds of questions to expect on the ASVAB
- when and where to take the ASVAB
- how career counselors and military recruiters will use your ASVAB scores
- what to do if you decide to join the military
- what kinds of jobs the military offers
- the benefits of a military career

And maybe most importantly for you at this point . . . how this book will help you max out your ASVAB score!

Asvab FAQs

WHAT, EXACTLY, IS THE ASVAB?

The ASVAB is an examination that's designed to help you—and others—see what kinds of jobs you may be good at. Called a "multi-aptitude battery," the exam is designed to measure your "aptitudes," or capabilities, at this point in your life. The ASVAB doesn't measure what kind of work you know how to do now. Instead, it measures your *readiness* to be trained in and become good at particular kinds of work—in other words, your career potential. The ASVAB measures capabilities that usually can help a person succeed in various kinds of careers.

The ASVAB is made up of a series of subtests designed to measure specific knowledge areas. Some of the subject areas listed below might look a little scary. For example, the automobile and shop knowledge subtest might look intimidating if you've never even picked up a wrench. But remember: The ASVAB is an *aptitude* test. There is no passing or failing grade. The exam is designed to help you learn more about your skills and abilities and help military placement personnel find the best job for *you*.

WHEN AND WHERE SHOULD I TAKE THE ASVAB?

You can take the ASVAB year-round at field stations around the United States. In addition, mobile teams offer the exam at high schools, where sophomores, juniors, and seniors may take it. It doesn't cost anything to take the ASVAB. In fact, the Department of Defense wants you to take the exam so that you can learn more about military career opportunities, and so that

recruiters can learn more about you—more on that below.

To learn where and when to take the ASVAB in your area, speak with your high school guidance counselor, or contact an Armed Forces recruiter.

HOW ARE MY ASVAB SCORES USED?

Two main groups of people will see your ASVAB scores: school guidance counselors and military recruiters. Guidance counselors use your scores to help you decide on a career path that seems right for you. Recruiters use the scores to learn of high school students who might be interested in joining the military. Here's an important note: Taking the exam doesn't obligate you in any way to join the armed forces. It can help you see what kind of jobs you'd be good at, whether in the armed forces and/or in the private sector workforce.

If you do join the service, your ASVAB scores will follow you throughout your military career. ASVAB scores are used not only to get you into the military, but also to qualify you to change jobs—if you decide to—once you're in. Let's say, for example, you join the service as an administrative clerk, but later decide you would like to become an air traffic controller. Military career counselors will check your AFQT to see whether you qualify to become an air traffic controller. That's why it's so important to take the ASVAB seriously, and study up. Your scores could impact your life for years to come.

IS THE ASVAB TEST HARD?

The ASVAB isn't "hard." Rather, it measures your knowledge of areas you've already studied. It also tests your speed and abilities in things like coding numbers and figuring out how simple machinery works. Below are the exact subject areas you'll find on the exam. We've also included examples of the kind of questions that will appear on each part of the test.

PRACTICE 5

1. **a.** *Expedite* means accelerate the process; to speed up.
2. **a.** *Fortune* means luck or fate.
3. **c.** To *absolve* means to exonerate or forgive, to free from blame or responsibility.
4. **d.** *Hoist* means to raise.
5. **d.** *Predictable* means foreseeable.
6. **c.** To *shore up* means to prop up and support.
7. **d.** *Simmering* means barely controlled; seething.
8. **b.** To *initiate* means to begin or cause to begin.
9. **c.** *Ravenous* means voracious, all-consuming.
10. **b.** *Uninhabitable* implies conditions are so terrible that life cannot be sustained there.
11. **b.** *Suppressed* means held in, repressed, not expressed outwardly.
12. **b.** To be *immersed in* means to be absorbed, engrossed, or involved in profoundly.
13. **a.** *Secular* means worldly, not specifically pertaining to religion.
14. **a.** *Haggle* means to bargain or dicker.
15. **d.** A *palpable* tension is so intense it almost seems a physical, tangible presence.
16. **c.** One meaning of *vicarious* is to experience or realize something through imaginative or sympathetic participation.
17. **c.** One meaning of *sprawl* is haphazard growth of a city, usually outward toward the suburbs.
18. **a.** *Exotic* means foreign, intriguing, having the charm of the unfamiliar.
19. **d.** To *meander* means to follow a winding course.
20. **b.** *Precarious* means dangerous.

PRACTICE 6

1. **a.** *Unity* means harmony or compatibility; *discord* means a lack of harmony.
2. **d.** *Detest* means to feel hostility toward, to strongly dislike; the opposite of detest is *admire*.
3. **b.** *Valiant* means acting with bravery or boldness; *cowardly* is the opposite.
4. **d.** *Lenient* means permissive, tolerant, or easygoing; *domineering* means exercising overbearing control.
5. **c.** *Tarnish* means to destroy the luster of; *shine* means to make bright by polishing.
6. **c.** *Mandatory* means containing a command; *optional* means having a choice.
7. **c.** *Chagrin* means distress caused by disappointment or failure; *pleasure* is the opposite of distress.
8. **d.** *Commence* means to begin; *terminate* means to end.
9. **a.** *Conscientious* means careful, cautious, and thoughtful; *careless* means not showing care.
10. **b.** *Deficient* means lacking some necessary quality; *complete* means having all necessary parts.
11. **c.** *Clarify* means to make clear; *obscure* means to make dark, dim, or indistinct.
12. **a.** To *grant* is to permit; to *deny* is to refuse to permit.
13. **d.** *Lucid* means clear.
14. **b.** *Impartial* means not partial or biased; *prejudiced* means biased.
15. **c.** *Judicious* means wise or prudent; *imprudent* means not prudent.
16. **a.** *Dissonance* means not in harmony.

17. **a.** *Erudite* means learned or possessing knowledge; *uneducated* means to lack training or knowledge.

18. **c.** *Amiable* means friendly; the opposite of friendly is *aloof*.

19. **c.** *Competent* means having adequate abilities; *inept* means incapable or not competent.

20. **b.** To *promote* is to advance someone to a higher rank or to advocate something; to *curtail* is to cut something short.

PRACTICE 7

1. **c.** *Requirement* means something obligatory; *option* means something chosen.

2. **a.** To *irritate* means to annoy; to *soothe* means to calm.

3. **d.** To be *punctual* means to be on time; to be *tardy* means to be late.

4. **c.** *Virtue* means a moral goodness; *vice* means a moral failing.

5. **d.** *Harmony* means agreement; *discord* means disagreement.

6. **a.** An *insult* is a gross indignity; a *compliment* is an admiring remark.

7. **a.** *General* means not limited to one class of things; *specific* means particular.

8. **b.** To be *fortunate* is to have good luck; to be *hapless* is to be unlucky.

9. **d.** *Imaginary* means unreal; *factual* means real.

10. **c.** To *demolish* means to tear apart; to *create* means to build.

11. **d.** *Notable* means unusual; *ordinary* means usual.

12. **a.** *Prim* means stiffly formal and proper; *outrageous* means shocking.

13. **b.** *Prosperous* means rich or affluent; *destitute* means very poor.

14. **b.** *Absorb* means to take in or consume; to *repel* is to reject or force away.

15. **d.** To be *critical* is to be important or vital to something; to be *trivial* is to be unimportant.

16. **b.** *Nimble* means quick and light in motion; *sluggish* means slow or inactive.

17. **a.** *Tranquil* means peaceful; *agitated* means disturbed or excited.

18. **c.** *Sprightly* means lively; *dully* suggests a lack or loss of keenness or zest.

19. **c.** *Infantile* means childish, *mature* means grown up.

20. **d.** To be *impulsive* is to be swayed by emotion or to make rash decisions; to be *cautious* is to show forethought.

21. **c.** *Amiable* means friendly; the opposite of friendly is *aloof*.

22. **c.** *Competent* means having adequate abilities; *inept* means incapable or not competent.

23. **b.** To *promote* is to advance someone to a higher rank or to advocate something; to *curtail* is to cut something short.

PRACTICE 8

1. **a.** To be *prudent* is to exercise good judgment; to be *rash* is to show ill-considered haste.

2. **b.** To *retain* is to keep or hold; to *release* is to let go.

3. **c.** *Scant* is meager; *copious* is abundant.

4. **b.** To be *steadfast* is to be fixed or unchanging; to be *fickle* is to be capricious.

5. **b.** To be *stringent* is to be rigorous or severe; to be *lax* is to be lacking in rigor or strictness.

6. **c.** To be *subjective* is to be influenced by one's own emotions or beliefs without strict regard to evidence in the outside world; to be *unbiased* is to be objective or impartial.

7. **d.** To be *succinct* is to be concise; to be *verbose* is to be wordy.

8. **a.** To be *tedious* is to be tiresome; to be *stimulating* is to be exciting.

9. **b.** To be *uniform* is to be consistent or the same as another or others; to be *diverse* is to have variety.

10. **d.** To be *wary* is to be on guard or watchful; *careless* is the opposite of watchful.

11. **d.** The adjective *novel* means new or not representing something formerly known; the adjective *old* means having lived or existed for a long time.

12. **a.** A *fallacy* is a false or mistaken idea, or trickery; a *truth* is something which conforms to the facts.

13. **d.** To *exonerate* means to clear from accusation or guilt, to *blame* is to accuse.

14. **d.** *ubsequent* means coming after or following, *previous* means coming before.

15. **c.** To be *nonchalant* means to have an air of easy indifference; to be *concerned* means to be interested and involved.

16. **b.** To *excise* means to remove; to *retain* means to keep.

17. **a.** To *disperse* means to scatter; to *gather* means to collect in one place.

18. **b.** *Prevarication* means evasion of the truth; *veracity* means truthfulness.

19. **b.** *Mirth* means merriment; *solemnity* means seriousness.

20. **b.** To *liberate* means to release; to *restrain* means to deprive of liberty.

PRACTICE 9

1. **a.** To *orient* means to adjust to; to *confuse* means to mix-up.

2. **d.** To *levitate* means to rise and float; to *sink* means to go under the surface.

3. **c.** To *pacify* means to calm; to *excite* means to stir up.

4. **c.** To be *plausible* is to be likely; to be *unbelievable* is to be unlikely.

5. **b.** *Avidly* means characterized by enthusiasm and vigorous pursuit.

6. **c.** *Meekly* means not violent or strong; *forcefully* means powerfully.

7. **a.** *Complacent* means self-satisfied or unconcerned.

8. **b.** To be *ambiguous* is to be equivocal or obscure; to be *certain* is to be definite or fixed.

9. **a.** To *esteem* is to have favorable regard; to *disrespect* is to lack courteous regard.

10. **c.** To be *eloquent* is to be fluent; to be *inarticulate* is to be unable to speak with clarity.

11. **a.** A *deterrent* prevents or discourages; *encouragement* inspires or heartens.

12. **d.** *Hierarchical* means classified according to rank, from low to high; egalitarian means all are equal, without rank.

13. **d.** Someone who is *impertinent* is rude; someone who is *polite* is courteous.

14. **c.** To be *ludicrous* is to be absurd; to be *reasonable* is to be rational.

15. **b.** To be *archaic* is to be ancient or outdated; to be *modern* is to be up to date.

16. **d.** *Sullen* means gloomy or dismal; *jovial* means very happy.

17. **a.** To be in *awe* of something is to admire it; to have *contempt* for something is to consider it worthless.

18. **b.** *Taut* means extremely tight; *relaxed* means not tense.

19. **a.** To *rile* is to upset; to *appease* is to pacify or satisfy.

20. **d.** To *mar* is to damage or deface; to *repair* is to restore or fix.

PRACTICE 10

1. **d.** An *intrepid* person approaches a challenge without fear, which is the opposite of *fearful*.

2. **a.** *Methodical* means careful or in a planned manner; *erratic* means having no fixed course.

3. **d.** *Latent* means present but not active; *active* is the opposite.

4. **a.** *Affable* means pleasant and at ease; agreeable.

5. **c.** *Trepidation* means fear; the opposite would be *fearlessness*.

6. **a.** *Auspicious* means something taken as a sign promising success; the opposite is *unpromising*.

7. **c.** *Militant* means engaged in warfare or combat; *pacifistic* means engaged in peace and diplomacy.

8. **b.** *Furtively* means done stealthily or secretively.

9. **d.** *Entice* means to attract by arousing hope; *repel* means to drive away.

10. **c.** *Ingenuous* means noble, honorable, natural, or candid; the opposite would be *calculating*.

11. **b.** To be *ostentatious* is to be showy and boastful; the opposite would be *humble*.

12. **a.** *Endorse* means to approve; *condemn* means to disapprove.

13. **c.** *Accede* means to express approval or give consent; *disapprove* means to express disapproval.

14. **b.** *Copious* means plentiful; *meager* means deficient in quality or numbers.

15. **b.** *Ambivalence* is uncertainty as to which approach to follow; *decisiveness* is having the power or quality of deciding.

16. **b.** *Divergent* means differing from a standard; *identical* means being the same.

17. **d.** *Pensive* means sadly thoughtful; thoughtless means lacking concern for others, careless, or devoid of thought.

18. **a.** One definition of *discernible* is visible with the eyes, so the opposite would be *invisible*.

19. **c.** *Vacillate* means to waver or hesitate; *resolve* means to deal with successfully.

20. **c.** *Abhor* means to regard with repugnance; *desire* means to long for or hope for.